Edu Small

Easy Cum, Easy Go

" if you know the journey, you know the outcome"

For the miss Scotland
Glasgow Lynette, the
lady of the most beatifu
pic's
Lots of reading pleasure

Edevsl

A CIP catalogue record for this title is
available from the British Library.

ISBN: 978-1-80074-741-8

First Published in 2022

Printed in Poland by Ridero

"Easy cum Easy go"

FOR THE LOVE OF MONEY IS A ROOT OF ALL KINDS OF
EVIL. SOME PEOPLE, EAGER FOR MONEY, HAVE
WANDERED FROM THE FAITH AND PIERCED
THEMSELVES WITH MANY GRIEFS."

About the Author

This book was except for the last few pages entirely written in prison without ghost-writer or help, just my memory and a hundred or so pens. And because I spent a total of several thousand days behind bars in 3 different countries, I had plenty of time for it. One page every day, occasionally two if I was in my element maybe three

I decided to put my experiences on paper after I shared an old story in the working premises of the jail with a fellow inmate about a drug transport, this guy raved about my story. That same evening, I started writing, some of the stories are very detailed and there are people who have questions about that, all I can say is that when you have had a specific experience in your life that is memorable, they also say is "etched in your memory" you remember much more than you expect.

Sometimes I couldn't squeeze out more than like one page, then I just didn't remember, it was empty and the next day in the yard with a note block and a pen I continued. Everything and I say emphatically everything in this writing is true, if I didn't remember something I skipped sometimes the entire story, however, to protect the identity off certain individuals some of the names or initials and a few locations are fictional.

I wanted to keep it "pure" so that no one can say in a later stage that this or that was made up, If so, that would discredit the entire book.

Some stories are illustrated with newspaper articles, not substantiated by the way, nothing special, press releases from the Police seldom have anything to do with the truth, Insiders know that, the police only leak information to the press that fits into their narrative.

Index

"You are a product of how you are raised"

- Dan Peña

They call it the "mattress" the area where I grew up, a few kilometers from the most expensive zip codes in the Netherlands, they call it the mattress because its slightly higher than the surrounding areas, and slightly higher is a lot in a flat country like Holland,

I was doing excellent from birth, but everything started to get complicated from the moment my memory ability started to work.

With a mum who is bipolar and a dad who is an alcoholic life isn't easy, starts of a bit cliché and I do realize that there are thousands of kids who have to deal with neglect and abuse, still, ide like to give you an idea where I came from because the way you are brought up will determine for a big part who you become in adult life, and the more boxes a person ticks off during your youth like, neglect, abuse, in short growing up an unbalanced environment the bigger the chance is that you will develop an addiction or even multiple ones as I did, and my addictions have all to do with a part of the book's title, understandably the "easy go" part.

I aspire that the book particularly appeals to people who are struggling with addictions, or maybe there will be some who recognize themselves while reading it and are in the process of developing an addiction.

After all, like the youngest heavy weight world champion in history Mike Tyson once said *"we are all teachers and pupils, we all learn from each other, the world is one big school"*

Any serious addiction is extremely harmful, physically, socially and financially, because whether you earn or save up 1500 EU, or 150,000, or like me generated roughly somewhere around 12 million, with an addiction it is guaranteed gone.

I grew up in a typical middle-class family, nothing fancy, not a big villa, but an ordinary terraced house

The seven of us were a large family, my brother and sisters all born in the '60s, with more or less one year difference between us. Although we lacked nothing for the outside, the reality was that behind the facade it was a mess, mum and dad only argued, I never heard them talk respectfully to each other nor about each other

There was no cohesion at all in the family, there was a large dining table with 6 chairs in the living room whereas far as I can remember we didn't eat together once

One sat with his food in the kitchen and the other with a plate of custard in her or his bedroom. Our dad was a heavy alcoholic with gambling problems and it happened more than once that I had to walk back home because he got stuck in the pub drinking and gambling, and after drinking 8 cans of coke and hearing 8 times *"we go in five minutes just order a glass of cola"* I had enough of it and walked back home 6 km and this as a 5- or 6-year-old boy, really not much older because I just didn't step in his car anymore

Our mum never got diagnosed being bipolar but in hindsight, with her severe shifts in mood and energy it was quite clear she suffered from it, and not only she, we all did, either way, she was not at all " up to the job"', physical violence or sexual abuse has been spared us, except for a few times I received a beating with mum's wooden slippers, but as far as psychological neglect concerned, we were not short of anything. One word pops into my head....love-less.., I can't remember, for example, that my mother once took me on her lap and 'stroked my head' that mama bear love that I craved so much that in later life it became one of the things that always impressed me deeply, even gave me goosebumps, when for example I saw my girlfriend taking her kids one by one on her lap and asked them in a very loving way how their day had been.

Much later I found out that both of my parents had also fallen short, many traumas and sadness, what you don't receive can hardly be passed on I think. Don't blame them either, it makes no sense, our father is long dead and buried, and mother has been placed into a care home at the time of writing and does not remember where she lived for the last 40 years of her life.

My mother "loved" nicking stuff, she was a kleptomaniac so to say, after she was arrested several times for shoplifting while she was being held at the police station two detectives came to search our house including my bedroom and asked me what I got from my mother lately, I pointed to a pile of underpants.

You probably think of such a nine or ten-year-old boy you do not confiscate his bit of clothes?

Still, those two coppers took everything with them, except one pair of pants, one sweater and the pile of underpants in question, I think this has laid part of the foundation for why I have an intense dislike for authorities today.

My mother always gave me Levi Strauss trousers, jackets, nice V-neck sweaters and polo shirts from La costa, clothes make the man.

That's always been the case, thanks mummy, even if it was stolen, you nicked it with love.

Because our mum regularly got caught shoplifting my sisters were eventually placed out of our home in a foster family and shortly before my brother had moved to a boy's boarding school

After being unemployed for years, my father was offered a job in the far East and me and my mother stayed behind, we were water and fire my mum and me, I was about 14 had just completed the first year of secondary school, and "failed" and ended up in the Lower Technical School

I didn't enjoy that technical school either, in the beginning, I skipped class for the first hour because sleeping felt more important, this quickly turned into hours, and soon I only attended in the afternoon, was also called to the director's office and there he threatened he would inform my parents and have a hearty conversation about me, I thought you'd do what you want, my mother has lost all control over me, if she ever had it, and don't believe my mother has any aspirations to win it back.

I was a loose cannon of about 15 years old. I did exactly what I wanted, got up when I wanted, went to bed when I wanted, ditto with an asterisk for coming home and leaving.

Got attracted to certain characters because one of my best mates was a tall blond boy with freckles, a good fighter, the strongest boy in the class or perhaps in the entire school, named Albert Abbenhuis, aka Appie. Under that name he was a few years later in all the headlines, not for a day, but for years, according to the police he had robbed a series of banks and supermarkets through the whole country, but things got completely out of hand at a supermarket in Oosterbeek.

The story was when he and two others entered the supermarket armed with riot guns, for unclear reasons two supermarket employees were killed with a shot in the neck and a third who tried to flee got shot in his back, leaving him in a wheelchair for the rest of his life.

Justice set up a task force and after extensive investigations ended up at Appie A, and two others among them Bobby B, who I also vaguely knew, and one Piet B. When the soil got too hot for Appie, he fled to Chile which had no extradition treaty with the Netherlands and converted to Jehovah, was to no avail even if he had converted to an Eskimo, 4 years after the robbery in 1993 he was extradited and sentenced to life in prison, that's where he is up to this day

It has the name in the rest of Holland to be "posh" this mattress where I grew up, but long before anyone had heard of liquidation processes and Moroccan mafia, friends of mine also were murdered in the mattress, strangely enough on one Saturday night in September 1986, two boys got murdered whom I both knew well.

Michael Poyé who literally until recently lived a stone's throw from me and Moustapha Satout, coincidental because both cases had nothing to do with each other, Moustapha made some burnouts with his BMW 735 in front of a coffee shop and got a bullet in his head from a stressed-out neighbor, and Michael was stabbed to death by a skinhead at the train station, Michael had an illegal FM transmitter just like me, and Moustapha was the first ever to show me a "sample" of hash.

I calculated that I have heard this news 19 times in the next 25 years, 14 by gun violence, two stabbed to death, 2 completely disappeared from the face of the earth, and one likely by strangulation. (Body was found 6 years later) Some I knew well, some very well, went even to some of their funerals, always very busy events, funerals of murdered people, post mortem no lack of friends.

I developed as a nasty piece of work, robbed everything lose and stuck, when the moped time came, I bought an old one and stole one with which I brightened up mine, until I got stopped by the old bill in the center, had to put my moped on the sidewalk and while the police inspected the moped exactly there where I got stopped a girl walks out from a butcher's shop with a butcher's jacket who inspects my moped from close by, and she suddenly yells *"hey that's my headlight!!"* she recognized her headlight because there was a dent in the chrome rim, well there I went, to the station, and during a search, they found a stolen frame from a Yamaha and some parts from a zundapp

Appie extradited from Chili

Spent a few days at the police station, was brought before a judge and later had to appear in court

In December 83 when I was just a few months into 17 I went into military service at the AFMTS, Air Force Military Training School in Nimwegen and joined the Air Force Security Corps, in itself nice training, shooting with UZI, FAL, FALO, throwing hand grenade(s) was then assigned to the 12th Group Guided Weapons in Vorden near Osnabruck in Germany, guarding Nike missiles, Americans inner parameter, we Dutch outer ring, guarding shelters and stored in those shelters laid a lot of missiles, many with nuclear warheads, could be recognized by a red top, (wasn't warhead itself) this was for recognition during surveillance, surveillance that was extreme just like my "work" which was extremely monotonous, from watchtower to watchtower, one hour in one tower and another hour in other, and at the weekends 12-hour shifts, until I had enough of it and after a few months "fled" to the border area and lived there for a month or so. Eventually due to lack of money, among other things, went back to my mum where the roof went off, quarrels everyday, the police came regularly and eventually they called in a social worker who ensured that I was at the top of the waiting list for a council apartment. I was quickly offered a house in the center of the village, That's where delinquency took on more serious forms, from tricks with angling in mailboxes and ordering stuff on other people names, falsifying cheques and joyriding with stolen cars and soon after deliberately stealing cars to do "jobs", Saab 900 Turbos were favorable, fast, easy to nick because the ignition is in between seats, so you could easily pull the cylinder out with a dent/lock puller, screwdriver in it, and off you go

Of course, this had to go wrong one day, which it did when me and the brothers B. stole an Opel Senator and went to a lingerie store in a village nearby we emptied it and drove with the loot to Amsterdam where we put it on a drink and when the money ran out in the early morning hours we tried to sell some of the lingerie to customers in a pub, of course with labels and prices still on it, my mother always said "your traitor never sleeps" and surely the cafe owner had called the police, because suddenly 5 coppers stood in the bar, around the corner the Opel senator was parked with loot in it, case closed, I disappeared for a while in the old prison of Leeuwarden, a kind of fortress, accumulation of cases and the Judge thought it was enough After returning from captivity I was closely watched by the local old bill, could not turn around or i was stopped, especially at night when they had spotted me I immediately had a tail in the shape of an undercover car or one of their regulars, an Opel Ascona with bells and whistles on it

"Size thirteen"

At one point I had my eye on a new Timberland store in the area, were very fashionable those shoes at that time, I saw at the back there was a dark red door, i just couldn't tell how many locks there were on the door, it was a blind door that could only be opened from the inside.

So I went to the store and actually bought a pair, burgundy red, with leather laces, so when I tried the shoes I asked the kid who worked there if he could grab a brown pair and as soon as he was inside the storage I "coincidentally" put my head into the storage to ask if he also had a light brown pair, meaning was to catch a glimpse of the inside door, and yes..... a lock in the middle, a bit a heavy one, but only in the middle.

I borrowed a combo from my neighbor, because I really couldn't do anything with my car. I parked near the door, crowbar in between, little by little, work up, once in between, pull it full, leverage, kawangggg!!!! The door was open, heard a high-pitched alarm going off and blindly grabbed as many boxes as possible and filled the combo, then drove combo to the other side of the street and parked it. Only when I parked did I hear the main alarm go off.

With a big detour I walked back home and picked up the combo the next evening. I had at somewhere between 30 to 40 pairs of timberlands, almost all women's shoes, and of the men I only had size twelve, twelve and a half and thirteen. So nothing for myself, ladies were all gone in no time, twelve too, but size twelve and a half and thirteen were complicated.

When I read it all back, I was a bit of a dickhead, I have to admit, but I have to add a comment, I always worked, I've had countless jobs since I left school, So i didn't just mess around, we called it also "extra earning." I had given my sister a few pairs of the Timberlands, and she asked me later if I had any left in terms of women's shoes I say "no sister, only men size boat twelve and a half and thirteen, sister pointed out to me that her boyfriend had size thirteen and was fond of timberlands, knew the man somewhat, met him once at a birthday, a man with Jewish background from Brooklyn New York who owned a number of coffee shops in the red light district in Amsterdam, i thought coffee shops was something for the hippies at the time, and found the man somewhat arrogant.

But I had to get rid of those shoes, so I went to Amsterdam with a big bag of shoes, once there he greeted me in his place right in the middle of the red-light district and he asked me to come downstairs where there was kitchen.

He tried on a few pairs, looked through the bag and took them all, except those that were double, and I was asking little already, twenty% of the shop price, but it wasn't enough for the man. The man wanted to pay fifteen % because he took almost all of them was his argument.

"ok friend, take them" I said, I put like six hundred in my pocket and because I didn't want to go back with the last five pair of shoes size thirteen which I probably couldn't sell anyway, so I told him he could have the remaining five pair as a present. he liked this, offered me a beer and asked me a question that apparently intrigued him and would ask me many times after, the question was whether if he had bought say two thirds of the shoes if I had also given the rest, *"'who knows'"* I replied, so thi0s was clearly not a satisfying answer for him.

After talking about small things, he asked me….*"besides robbing shops...you do anything else??"* no I replied, while he was standing behind the bar and fiddling around with the cash register, then he came back to me... *"you don't feel like working here? - "security"? I* have to say that I've done sports all my life, I've weighed around hundred kg since I was twenty, I'm stocky build so they say, he offered me ten guilders an hour, i agreed right away, he asked if I wanted to come back the next day and he would explain what the intention was, he already hinted that it was not about ordinary doorman's work, but more to keep an eye on people, sort of "counter surveillance" so follow people who followed our movements, people he would point out to me, and I had to leave the rest to my gut feeling .

The next day he explained to me that the intention was to keep out at least the "typical" street dealers which were easy to recognize, but keeping in mind that Amsterdam was a completely different city than it is now, Amsterdam center in the 80s you couldn't walk around drunk in the middle of the night, without a considerable chance of being robbed, it was also teeming with dealers, all had their own corner or bridge, north Africans especially Algerians, Antilleans and Surinamese all had their own derision, but he saw much more damage resulting from a partly regular clientele, characters who spent hours zipping on an orange juice and who kept an eye on the stairs that went down to an office.

According to him they only sit there to hijack clients from the shop, and then took me down past stock of crates and barrels of beer, and tucked in between the crates he opened a sort of camouflaged door to a "secret" office maybe twelve square feet in size with a small escape hatch into a patio and there again was another gate that opened into one of the intervening alleys. *"This is the beating heart of the shop"* my brother-in-law said

Those tourists who ate space cake and drank a beer were nice he said, but the real money was made in that cellar, there was a desk in it with a few drawers containing a kilo or so of hash and weed , all samples, later I learned what it all was, Lebanon in oval shape with those cotton pink or blue bags, ketama, French newspapers, border afghan, power afghan, charas manali, skunk, purple sense and so on.

Of course there were also dealers who walked around with a menu, such as a booklet with folding transparent flaps, depending on the days / holidays and weekends, about 1500 to 2000 guilders a day was sold, he explained further, but the real slammers were made with customers who bought from a few hundred grams to say 25 kg, and more, for those he had access to a garage right in the center where if they requested the merchandise could be built into any car.

A new world opened up for me, in the middle of the red-light district all sorts of characters and nationalities came over the floor, drunks, thugs, pickpockets, scammers, whores with or without a pimp, motorcycle club related figures, happy people, psychological confused people, ugly people and beautiful people in all colors and sizes, beautiful, the city of Amsterdam.

The Coffee shop where it all started, Rick's Cafe

And because off all the coffee shops it was like a Mecca for many people from around the world who liked to smoke a spliff, and not the most ordinary of public, it was buzzing with people, at that time there were about 300 windows where girls worked in shifts 24/7, it was busier in some alleys than in the zoo after the birth of a baby gorilla so to speak and the lack of interest off politics and police to intervene involving soft drugs made it a real Walhalla for people who were in the trade, but what i didn't realize than that this was all just temporary, from mid eighties till about 1998, after that through legislation slowly but surely the red light district and the coffee shops were decimated

I didn't shine as a doorman for long, maybe I didn't take my job seriously, I was much more busy discovering my new world, sure street dealers could recognize a small child, they did not come in, I also drew customers' attention to not put their bags next to the table unattended because in them days a junky just ran by and it would be gone, and there were some customers who showed to obviously interest in the stairs that went to the cellar i asked them politely to F&*#k of, and in case there were customers downstairs, if they left I escorted them to where their hotel or car was.

But the real "customer hijackers" came from completely different corners I later found out. They were real regulars who sophisticatedly pretended to be your friend, or from what I also experienced later, (even your best mates themselves)

"Sparta with auxiliary engine"

Since my brother-in-law was occasionally difficult with paying, and often made problems about the number of hours I worked, I suggested to him to combine my work with selling from the menu, so say porter/dealer, he agreed, so quickly after I became a dealer from which he expected to keep order and keep out the competition for the same percentage that other dealers got, so basically I got nothing for the "security" job he hired me for.

These dealers were supplied, and we are talking about three coffee shops by a little Australian man who lived somewhere in the Jordaan he came by one of the first motorized Sparta bicycles, every now and then I had to go there because the man often had problems with his bowels, after he couldn't come by again for the umpteenth time, my brother-in-law wanted to visit his home to see what was really going on with the man. Once at the door, it took quite some time before he pressed the buzzer to open it, saw my brother-in-law already looking irritated, we went upstairs and once inside the Australian was clearly nervous, he hadn't expected my brother-in-law to be there, he apologized that he was in the shower, i saw my brother-in-law clearly feed his eyes while communicating with him in a somewhat arrogant way, he was good at that, being arrogant *"so you are sick, aint you"* he says as he opened the shower door and continued talking to him, then proceeding to bedroom which he opened without asking, *"who the fuck is this?"* I hear him yell, I took a glimpse into the bedroom, i saw a woman in bed, and could only qualify her, let's say; as a street heroin junky, my brother-in-law was clearly not amused by the whole spectacle, and listed everything he had observed " *listen you little prick"* ", by the way everything in English, always in English he understood Dutch very well, but never spoke it, this was part of his act, he went on to the Australian, *"you say you're sick, I'm downstairs waiting for minutes in front of your fuckin door, you apologize for being in the shower, well your hair is wet, yes, but your shower is dry",* he says, while running his finger along the edge of the coffee table and then against his tongue, he continues," *you didn't wash that dirty little body of yours while I waited, you were wiping traces of the party you had with that filthy whore laying in your bed, and you cleaned the table because there was coke on it, further more you have 25 large of trade laying here, my money! " You filthy little cock!" 'And last but not least you have a whore laying in your bedroom 2 meters from the safe where MY trade is, " give me the fucking keys of the safe, NOW!!* 'He says, impressive speech I must say, he didn't give a shit, stunned the little Australian man gave the keys, muttering "*but, but, i am* blah blah...my brother in-law emptied the safe and books in it and immediately added in an unmistakable way that he was no longer welcome in any of his shops, we went down the stairs with a bag full of trade, scales, packaging material, cutting boards and cheese knives once arrived at my car he says *"you want a new job?"* So I went up the ladder, got a percentage of turnover from the three stores, which would be at least 1000 guilders per week, sometimes increased to 2000 per week during holidays, an astonishing amount of money in those days, especially for a 23-24 year old boy, have to say it was seriously a job and a half, was really as busy as give it a name, rented a house right in the heart of the center on the Nieuwendijk 103 2th floor, bit of an mistake because it was next to an alley called karnemelksesteeg and later on I noticed it got used as an urinal, stronger than that, when it was "Queens day" there was a pool of piss two inches deep.

Bought my first mobile phone, a Carvox 4000, was in the days people looked at you with a phone like you were an alien, they were only sold at business centers, with extra battery, an interface for an answering machine and a boat antenna, the phone cost around FL 8000, - rock-solid old-fashioned guilders. Every now and then I also helped brother-in-law with his big customers in his garage on the short Keizerstraat just behind Newmarket, he had German customers, Swedish, a Swiss and a few Irish, mostly I had to change the money at the border exchange office, and help pack and install the merchandise in cars, my brother-in-law preferred not to get his hands dirty, furthermore the big quantities were all arranged by a dud from Corsica, you could mostly find him in that small office that my brother-in-law had shown me the first day, the Corsican had the connections for purchasing, although almost all these suppliers were exclusively Dutch at the time.

First phone on the market, not only you're interesting for the birds, but in general people looked at you as if you were from space

The Corsican lived together on the canal with a Dutch girl with an Indonesian background, it was he who also exercised a controlling function over the dealers, did purchases for shops and for large customers, in fact he was in charge of the soft drugs department, the amounts that were earned on those large customers were exorbitant, I mean around 650 to 1000 guilders per kilo, and to think that every 10 days or so there was a client at the door like that, you are talking easy about a quarter of a million a month, sometimes I got a couple of grand extra when he needed help, the Corsican got a percentage, was around

20%, the rest for brother-in-law, no wonder the man from New York had shops here.

Well, this Corsican also had a problem, besides talking English like inspector Clouseau, he had a facial pain, a nerve in his face sometimes gave him brutal pain, I noticed that every now and then when we did the accounting.

Went to all kinds of doctors but nothing helped, eventually he went to Switzerland to have his face operated, he would be gone for 2 weeks and i would take his place until he got back.

Those 2 weeks turned into 3, then 5, I can remember well that I was sitting downstairs in the office with my brother-in-law and he explained to me how to improve the bookkeeping, he emphasized that it was very important, and always saying *"remember numbers don't lie, people do"* and at exactly on that moment that Corsican called, my brother-in-law spoke to him, and i could conclude from the conversation the Corsican was postponing his return again, *"are you kidding me? and you expect your percentage also?"* I heard my brother in law say, blunt and arrogant as always, he continues *"listen, stay there in Switzerland, you are not indispensable here I'll go on with the show with the Dutch kid"* [me]

I couldn't believe it, but the man had just given me a key position in his stores, one that could make me a millionaire

……………. if I had just behaved myself …………..

Of course I had proven in those 5 weeks that I could do it, I also found out later that I caught smaller percentages than the Corsican, so the knife cut both ways for my brother-in-law, I didn't have the impression that he liked that Corsican anyway, I could tell the way he talked about him, I actually wonder if he liked anyone at all, it was more all about him, and his money, that was extremely important to him, the man earned lots of money, but was in general too frugal to shed a tear.

I did learn a lot from him, I really appreciated his business acumen, being an entrepreneur.

At that time I was responsible for 3 shops, each shop had 5 dealers working in shifts so pl/min 15 dealers, the problem was that I simply couldn't handle it all, I had already had a hyperventilation attack in those 5 weeks, very strange if you experience that for the first time in your life, very frightening, also ended up in hospital because of it, almost kicked the dashboard out of the taxi when I pulled one on the street, seriously i thought I was having a heart attack, and the cab had to speed through all the red traffic lights.

[Hyperventilation is rapid or deep breathing, usually caused by anxiety or panic. This over breathing, as it is sometimes called, may actually leave you feeling breathless.] source Mayo Clinic

Once in hospital breathing with a plastic bag and nothing to worry about, but still it had to deal with the fact that I started at 09.00, ok, sometimes an hour later, but until closing time I stayed until 2:00 am on weekends, I worked 14 hours a day sometimes, and all-day walking in between those shops, 2 in the warmoesstraat and flagship on the OZ Voorburgwal.

Someone had to come and do my job, cutting and supplying the shops, and we also needed someone for security, say the "counter surveillance" my brother-in-law and I agreed on.

First a kid nicknamed Flip who I got on well with, a boy who I lets say lured away from another coffee shop by paying him better, boy of Spanish descent was a machine in recognizing a piece of hash, , he crumbled the stuff, burned the material and managed to accurately determine the price at 50 guilders per kilo, this lad was a real asset to the business.

Not long after my brother-in-law himself came up with someone to do the security, he had already met him and he wanted us to sit down together. I remember very well the first time I met this dude, he called himself GG, like my brother-in-law from the US, guy in his 50s, a bit of an oriental look, came from a southern state, Alabama or south Carolina, had such a redneck accent, hefty muscular guy with a weird look, and when i looked at him closely I saw where that strange look came from, the man had one glass eye, and on the same side of his face a kind of dimple in his skull, smiling, firm handshakes on arrival and departure, and that smile again, which was just as fake as his teeth.

Once he was gone my brother-in-law explained that he was a Vietnam veteran, and that oriental look came from his native roots.
He had native Indian blood in him.

I didn't feel anything with the man, but my brother-in-law had to have that man, he had already had several quarrels with a few members of a motorcycle club who at that time were in charge in Amsterdam, there had to be paid, protection, did many bar owners around there, pay, that word was not exactly in my brother-in-law's dictionary.

I thought that GG must have bluffed his way through with his elbows, how is the man going to take on that motorcycle club on his own? I advised my brother-in-law to pay those few thousand a month to get rid of the bullshit, he totally disagreed, and said, " *when you start with paying them, they got you by the balls, there is no end in sight,* and he looked at me like i was a fag turd, maybe that was true in hindsight , but after all i was only a kid at the time.

In any case, my brother-in-law rented a house for him in a side street of Oude Hoogstraat, the Bethaniëndwarsstraat, a few hundred meters from the shop.

He immediately started patrolling between the shops, what I have to admit is that the man had a high effect of "don't fuck with me" standing there in front of the shop with his arms folded, but I still didn't have a click with him.

 My brother-in-law apparently had a lot of confidence in him, because he wanted me to give all the stock to him, he was going to supply the stores I would solemnly do the purchases and serve the major customers that was the man's plan, they were his stores so i put me down to the man's plan.

Brought all the small items to GG as requested, once there in Bethaniënstraat he opens the door, he lived on the first floor, come into his house he literally had all his walls covered with covers of the magazine 'soldier of fortune' also here and there

A few hundred of these on your wall makes you defo a nutter

a poster of a playmate, but really a hundred of those covers of guys with machine guns, I stole everything out on his table and grab a list to explain what is what , how to cut and to weigh items, meantime, that dude is doing push-ups , 30 40 ,50 times, even with one arm every now and then, totally toned body, he didn't drink or smoke, I write a few things down, make copies of everything, then he starts showing off with his nunchaku sticks in front of the mirror, with a lot of verbal noise, WHO, WAA, TSAA,

I think what a weirdo, my brother-in-law wanted me to do the bookkeeping with him once a week, I really don't think so, not going to happen, I must think of another solution, decided on the spot that I was going to do it differently, I only wanted a list and the envelopes from the shops, I didn't go into his house. The man gave me the creeps, maybe he did all that weird stuff to impress, so let's say to have a free hand, well in that case he achieved his goal.

Shortly afterwards the man earned his first stripes, I was not there myself, but he had caught a few guys who had tried to break open the slot machines on the top floor of the shop, must have made a big impression because everyone was talking about it in the shops, apparently he had kicked the two out in a very masculine way.

"Bad shawarma"

Finding good staff was not easy, now tourists who wanted to stay in Amsterdam ran the doors flat [Dutch saying for very busy place, many people] for a job behind the bar or dealer, just like students did, after a few years of walking between those shops I was in a short time from a provincial to someone who had an eye for someone who could be a dealer, woman or man, as a male dealer I preferred to have a bit of a hippie figure, if it was a woman, preferably a bit of an eccentric type, for example we had a Swiss girl working, talked 4 languages, full of tattoos, very attractive, a true sales machine, we also had a Canadian Caucasian dude with Rasta braids from Montreal, spoke fluent French and English, we had a German working and actually we had so many nationalities, except Dutch, never had a Dutchman, don't know why, usually I hired dealers who were introduced by an existing dealer, you always have some kind of certainty built into it, if he or she does something wrong, like stealing clients, or bring their own bags of 10 and 25 guilders, you can always call the dealer to account who brought him or her to you.

What I had learned from my predecessor, that Corsican, you had to take a good look at the turn over envelopes, because if a dealer had his own supplier and they 'separated" a customer from our store, a dealer will put 100% in his or her pocket, instead of the 20% which was agreed on, By now I knew how a hare ran because make no mistake a dealer who sold well and brought in larger customers could already earn thousands a week -when they were honest- but if they decided to cheat us, they could multiply that to easy 10 or even 20 thousand a week.

But I knew what was being converted on certain shifts, also that there was always a larger customer at each dealer so now and then, if there was a fixed line at a specific dealer, no spikes, no larger customers, something was wrong.

I tried to also keep an eye on their spending habits, clothes, where they lived, how much rent they paid, whether they always or often hang out with the same person, or worse, took that same person to the store, all indicators that you are getting shafted

If this was the case, I got an ace out of my sleeve and sent pseudo buyers along. I had a German, an Englishman and an Italian, all acquaintances who I had become friends with over the years, so we have regularly caught a dealer.

There was a Brazilian who worked in the Warmoesstraat, had not had larger customers for months, had meagre turnover, walked with shoes of 400 guilders, heard that he had parties in the Mazzo disco, then I thought it was time to lay a trap down.

Called my German friend and gave him clear instructions to say that he needed to pretend that he was interested in 20kg and that he needed a garage to build it into a car so to win some time and gave him a red Ferrari cap to wear.

I was waiting for him around the corner from the shop, when he came back he already had his thumbs up, he had taken the bait, he had made an appointment with the Brazilian the next day at 1pm in front of the tulip inn hotel, and my phone of course remained silent, it is supposed that if a larger customer walks in to the shop to call me directly, nada, nix, winka, I got you boy, by your Brazilian balls.

Well in the past they were just fired and maybe a few slaps, but I had the feeling now that G.G was there it could turn out differently, and it did.

The next day me and GG already stood there at 12.30 in front of the tulip inn, and yes, there came the Brazilian.

He saw us, he probably thought, shit, that's bad timing just when that customer comes here, *"hey how r u"?* .."*what are you up to*"? I asked, he said *"just waiting for an old friend"* then my blood was already boiling, .. *"Old friend"*? I say, *maybe a German old friend who wants to buy 20 kg?* While I take the red cap from under my sweater and put it on my head.

Then he knew his gig was over, got a complete pull-out, and the "sorry but I wanted to call you" stories didn't work either, with index finger to lips or a shhhht was enough,

GG gave him a hard pat with his flat hand on the back of his head with that Vietnam ring of his, and the tone was set, he the super underdog and we are clearly the dominant party, his name

was Raoul, *"come on Raoul, we go to your house" i* said, , , we walked up to his apartment which was very nearby and when he opened the lock, I heard in his pocket he still had a bunch of other keys.

In the apartment stood a sofa bed with a table with two chairs, a very tiny apartment.

He sat down very timidly and extremely nervous, *"you really live here? "* i asked, In the meantime GG went threw the wardrobe, threw everything on the floor, this apartment felt, smelled like a woman lived there, and that was what it was, only women's clothing from the wardrobes.

I called one of the stores and asked our manager Nico if he knew where he lived, *'somewhere east side of town'* he said, *"you are wasting our time Raoul, basically you are fucking us"* "GG asked him to get up and gave him unexpectedly a nasty hard blow in his stomach area, little Brazilian fell to the floor creeping from the pain, ¨ *and now you gonna show us your real house*¨ the boy could not even answer immediately, I have also been hit like that before, takes away all your air so i asked him to lay down on the sofa bed, and brought him a glass of water ¨*get yourself together Raoul, because we have to see your house*¨

... .¨ *Nico says you live in the east of town, so let's go there*¨ with tears running down his cheeks, he nodded a yes.

And because the kid still had to recuperate from the punch in his stomach GG continued to search, and yes, below the sink he found a box full of bags of weed and hash, exactly the same as ours, we had bags of ten guilders and 25 guilders, about 50 bags that I remember, most of 25 guilders, we found under his sink, me and GG studied them, wasn't our trade what was inside, GG agreed ¨*not ours*¨ this made me more pissed off, *ok Raoul, get up, we're going now to your apartment* ¨*don't fuck us again, because GG is very likely going to break a few bones*¨, looking very pathetic, he nodded a yes with his head again than we walked together towards the martyrs road, Raoul walked slightly bent with clenched teeth, we hailed the first available taxi, *gentlemen where is the journey going*? the driver asks with an unadulterated Amsterdam accent, Raoul with his half-cracking voice, "*towards Katendrecht*", the taxi driver.

44

gosh is there something wrong with that gentleman?" Yes I say ....." *his stomach, ... food poisoning¨* I quickly repeated in English for GG and the rat, , *"so we bring him to his house and get medicine¨* i continued to say, while driving I see the driver regularly looking in his mirror, so as not to give the man the impression that there was in fact an unlawful deprivation of liberty taking place, I ask the driver, *"is there actually a pharmacy in the* area?" he had to think for a moment, "*yes at the mill nearby*", I repeat that in English to GG and the rat ¨

And while I mess through Raoul's hair, saying, ¨*you shouldn't just eat a shawarma in any place my friend*˙ GG put it a bit over the top by saying, "*yeah that shawarma stuff is real bad for the stomach HA HA¨*and as always his big fake teeth laugh.

 Once there I gave the cabdriver a nice tip, and asked where that pharmacy was, just to feel, see if that man might smell there is something wrong,, I mean such a strange guy as GG a Brazilian who sits bent over all the time while moaning, and me, well are not an everyday crowd you get in your taxi, man starts with a whole explanation how to get there, interrupted him and say that I already knew where he meant, I believed that it was okay with the man.

"Keys *Raoul* " I say, we went in, he had an attic floor, once inside, nice apartment, with nice wooden floor in it, I immediately recognized those strange expensive shoes with those metal hard rock decoration nails in them , GG started just like with the previous apartment emptying draws, while Raoul still leaning forward, and saying *"I am so so sorry about this"* almost crying.

After opening some drawers and cupboards, we found a small 18,000 cash in a very striking double bottom of a drawer, this and all the trade we had found we naturally confiscated, GG ordered him to fill a suitcase with clothes - because following our plan he would go on a journey¨, the man was a terribly pathetic pile of person, had no idea, had genuine fear of death in his eyes, we then escorted him according to plan to the central station, bought one-way ticket to Paris with his own money and gave him 300 guilders extra , and waited on the platform for the train until it left with him in it, and gg made it clear to Raoul while we waited for the train that he could never ever come back to Amsterdam, which he seemed totally in agreement with, man was visibly relieved, he absolutely thought this was his last day on the planet

Our other coffee shop Hunters bar where the Brazilian worked

Everything went well in the following months, everyone was happy, stores ran about 150,000 per month in pieces, on top of that there was a going and coming of larger customers, profit from the larger deals, was between 200 and 400,000 per month , every weekend there were customers from all over Europe, even the world, one 10 kg, another 30, and really at that time, you could get the merchandise with a phone call at such a hash office where my brother in law had introduced me to. One kilo of Moroccan hash cost for example, 2100 guilders, there were some Germans who came in every couple of weeks who wanted 20 kilos and once we ended up in the basement, the movie started, samples on the table, many samples, they were overwhelmed, they really did not leave our bunker/basement without a bag of hash, and the shop with their money, I would not let them continue shopping, after all there was a lot of competition in the area, we really weren't the only ones so a deal had to and would come.

In any case, 2100 guilders for a kilo, were stickers on all the samples that corresponded with prices on a note, *"dreitausend diese",* (three thousand this one)I said, that German had a difficult look *"aba ist das in D-mark oder guilder?"* (is this d-mark or guilder)
"You have D-mark, don't you?".... *"Yes"* so 'D-mark then 'I said, that was around 3300 guilders, that German looked difficult, *"can you do it for less"?* I also gave him a difficult look and after a lot of difficult looking at each other at the end he paid 2850 DM each, was like 3135 guilders each, had the material tugged by having a hash office deliver it, they put it in the kitchen 3 meters further on, I picked it up as soon as i heard three bangs on the wall, trade inspecting, counting money and done, a good 20,000 guilders profit on Saturday afternoon.

These were no exceptions, as it was normal at that time, money came in like water, I was dining out every day including expensive wines the whole shebang in either the sushi bar in Okura, or in restaurant Vermeer, or Ciel Bleu also located in

Okura all the way upstairs, all places with Michelin stars at the time, clothes make the man, must have spent at least 50 k a year at famous clothes shop Tip de Bruin, the dude in charge Jaap was like a little happy boy when i came in to his shop, and that is still without the famous brand shops in the PC Hooftstraat and in the evening in the disco, the Richter, or the IT on the Rembrandtplein, and many times to finish the day in "style" i (we) finished off in one off the many brothels, was also at the time that I bought the Porsche 911 s4 from world kickboxing champion Rob Kaman and despite living large, I also saved money, had a sentry safe in my mother's attic between the roof where I had 580,000 guilders in it at a certain moment (not in a few months of course).

"Cutting a window frame"

My brother in law had taken over the adjoining building next to our flag ship, he wanted to turn it into an organic food shop, I didn't really believe in it, there were already so many restaurants in the area, kebab places, Gauchos, steak and fries, Indian, Chinese and so on, but perhaps the man was also far ahead of the time, there was nothing decent to eat, and in the early nineties hardly anyone had heard of ecological, organic food, so could go either way.

G.G started renovating there. Around this time I walked into our store one day and saw Martin from the prominent biker club sitting at the bar, who was reasonable smashed on the booze already, big guy with a beard, an ex marine, said to him and Tatiana a blond girl that worked behind the bar hello and went to my bunker as usual to do my work.

At one point i hear a lot of stumbling and screaming upstairs, I ran upstairs and i saw GG working martin outside who by the looks of it had his hand full of blood, Tatiana was standing behind the bar with a wet towel against her face, there was also some broken glassware on the bar and ground, and some blood splatter here and there.

Martin once outside was yelling at G.G who had his arms folded and looked with stoic face

I asked Tatiana what had happened, her version was that Martin, who was kind of a regular customer, was very drunk, made sexist remarks, that she went to the toilet and once she sat down somebody sprayed tear gas under the door.

Her eyes and face were bright red. According to her could only been one. Martin, she said, looked like it because there were only two tourists standing in the corner who looked shocked by the incident. Tatiana had called GG who did what he was hired for and Martin had smashed a glass and cut his hand in the process when GG asked him to leave, that's why the blood and broken glassware.

I saw Martin walk away across the bridge towards the "other place"

(bar from motor club in question) and I knew this story would get a tail.

Tatiana tried to pick up the pieces again by sprinkling a lot of water on her face. G.G went back to work in the new bar next door, and I went back to my little bunker. And yes, about fifteen to twenty minutes later I am called by Tatiana, *"come up quickly*!"

Once upstairs I see about eight to ten motor club characters in front off the door, Tatiana: *go and talk to them, they want to see GG! -"Where is that fucking American?* !! Martin shouts once I was outside, I said " *moment, he isn't here, maybe next door"*

So I walked into the bar where G.G was painting in the back, I found him on his knees, and he was in painterly terms," cutting a window frame", say sharply painting the edge of the window frame and wall.

I told him in a bit of an excited way mildly expressed , GG *"there like ten dudes waiting for you outside !!* "Now everyone reacts differently, but I will never forget his reaction, he did not give a kick, didn't even look at me ', quietly continued painting and said something like *"Oh yeah, is there a meeting of some sort? ", tell them i am coming,* and finished the stroke he was making with his brush, I walked out again and in the meantime there were even more motorcycle club members, i told them that he would come in a minute, I saw nothing in such a confrontation that could not be won, now both stores had an emergency exit, a small window in one, and a escape hatch in the other, but i walked into the dam street away from the bar, on the Dam square I called my brother-in-law and told them about what happened, my brother-in-law who lived 10 minutes away from there asked me to go back to the shop immediately and he would do the same, I knew that my brother-in-law had various firearms, and walked back to the store with lead in my shoes, once arrived I saw Brother in law's bike lying on the floor and saw him standing in front of the store, totally agitated. The angels were gone, walked in, the whole shop inside was smashed to pieces, all the glassware, liquor bottles, mirrors, and three televisions were shattered, there was literally 3 inches of glass behind the bar, Brother in law was not really approachable, Tatiana was sitting defeated on the back stairs and told me they kept asking about that American, and smashed the whole place in minutes, then brother in law came and yes he pulled his gun and what I think most of us would do, they made a run for it.. and GG was nowhere to be found apparently, disappointing, as cool as he was, I had not expected this from him.

My brother-in-law calmed down and quickly put things into perspective, *"fuck this, a few televisions, some glass work, clean up, call brewery for new glasswork and business as usual"* he said

I thought, well those angels will not come back today, they got their revenge for now and know that brother-in-law walks around with a piece, but of course the tone was set, they did not like him, he had threatened them with a firearm, *it was a fucking Jew* like they often said, obviously there was a tail here.

Later that evening I was called by GG, who asked where the "headquarter" of the angels was. I explained to him near the Amstel station and more or less how to get there. After the short conversation I thought, what does he want to do? ? I had him on a statue respect wise, he was not afraid of the devil, he always said *" i am living on borrowed time"*, but if you want to compete against a whole club on your own, you have to bring rocket launchers with you, besides that he had run off

The shop was open again around noon the next day, televisions new, glassware, as brother-in-law had said.

I was sitting on the terrace and who came whistling? the last one I expected ...... .that G.G I looked at him with a questioning look, .. and ??

"No problem man, talked with the president and some other members off the board of directors, all cool now"..

I think, ferfucksake, he went to the lion's nest by himself on his bicycle.

Came out again with his orange juice, and says, *"but the boss has a problem, they want to have a chat with him"*

Called him up and told the news, *"well I don't go to that fucking place" or something along those lines.*

Later they approached him somewhere nearby and said, "if you ever pull a gun on an angel again, you better use it"

With that, most of the storm had passed, my brother-in-law went shortly afterwards to Vermont where his parents lived and would stay away for a few weeks. for G.G we had rented another floor, because he got visit from his wife or whatever it was , sort of a dolly Parton type.

G.G at that time not only distributed the stock but also collected the envelopes, I only handled the larger customers, purchasing and staff.

Normally I would sit with G.G every week, go through the envelopes of which every service of each dealer was administration, of the number of bags of takeover, sale and transfer, these must correspond with each other, money had to be in it minus a percentage of dealer. Period

G.G did not give home, not 1 week, not 2 weeks, but did collect the envelopes every day, who was I to rage against that psychopath? and after about 3 weeks he avoided me, and therefore did not get money to do some shopping, the situation became dire. Dealers started to complain that they had a very limited menu and were missing out on customers.

I calculated that the man should have had like 80,000, more likely towards 100,000. Looking at the menus of the shops, normal 12 types, there were only 4, and turnover was almost gone, dealers received their guarantee wage of 50 guilders, this couldn't go on, I had already informed my brother in law several times, who in turn had contacted GG, but GG always told the same bullshit "all ok boss", "I sort everything "blah blah I told him he don' do fuck at all, he didn't even collect the envelopes anymore, because there was almost no money in them anyway.

"Backward kick brake"

Brother-in-law would take the first plane back to Schiphol. Once back it was also clear to him that the business was on its ass, there were already dealers who did not even turn their shifts anymore. We made an appointment in a restaurant at the height of Kadijk that looked exactly into the street of GG, we took a table at the window and decided to call him there. Brother-in-law called him with my phone because my dear brother-in-law was a little too tight to buy one himself (in those days a cellular phone cost a fortune) and I was half listening, he answered, _Hey efert my man! How r u !!_ he said enthusiastically, _No G. G its_ me A. i think we need to talk, GG replied *"about what boss? There is nothing to talk about"*..

``*Just leave me and my misses alone* "he said... I saw my brother-in-law looking irritated, and he speaks

"listen you fucking redneck, you have a shit load of money that belongs to me, and you are fucking up my business ...silence ... .

``*are you finished*"? *"Listen, boss, if you want to start like this, threatening me and my family, you, that Dutch kid (me) and Nico better watch out for any accidents from now on*¨

Man sounded cool, , scary almost, he hung up, I say to my Brother in law *listen, that money is gone, clearly, he no longer has any trade, we have to keep going, find someone else who can do his job, I can get credit at offices, and forget that GG,* and also told him that I had seen him smoke a base pipe, and yes that I had sucked it too.

What?? when was that?? why didn't the fuck you tell me?? I said it.s actually the first time for me but I could hardly sound the alarm on this GG because of a pot-blaming kettle black story so to say.

Once you have lifted a lid on such a story, people generally want to know everything, so had to bear my buttocks, and told him in general terms what had happened that evening, not pointing a finger on who sucked the pipe, but who was present that evening among them was Nico, our regular from the bar, my brother-in-law spoke to him a few days later. Like all addicts he pretended if it was nothing, now and then a little line, if there was some tiny bit left smoking a small, tiny pipe, as if it was the most normal little tiniest thing in the world, and yes GG also took a tiny suck from the pipe now and then.

Downplaying everything, typically I've noticed later in life for people with a drug problem that they don't see, or don't want to see the seriousness of.

Brother-in-law was disappointed, he said" *you have told me earlier, than i would have taken the precautions would have set him step by step on a side rail"*

I told him to forget about that man, he is a base pipe smoking psychopath who always says he lives on borrowed time.

Forget that guy, forget that cash, I can ask flip one of our house dealers to do his job, just start from zero again, the locations are there, and never lack of public

Brother-in-law agreed, but he muttered, *fuck this, I am not saying goodbye to a 100 grand*, and shook his head.

I don't know what happened between my brother-in-law and GG concerning interaction communication, but that it was escalating soon became clear.

I never called that psychopath again, he called me regularly, but I simply did not answer.

But my brother-in-law, on the contrary GG, called his house number day and night, cycled past his house, and then pontifically stood in front of the door, he did the same at the shops, and with the manager Nico on the canal, I also saw him cycle past, I was sitting on the terrace and just before closing time he drove past with a plastic bag with an object in it in his hand, very slowly and looking straight in my face without saying a word.

I thought what a total crazy nutter this man is, he has stolen 100 k from us and has an attitude as if we stole 200 k from him.

This game went on for weeks He had scared the manager to death by suddenly standing a meter away from him when he locked the door. He suddenly stood in front of him with an iron face, asking if everything was okay with him. The manager fled the city because of that

Fortunately, G.G did not know where I lived, I was also extremely alert, constantly looking around me when I went to or came from home.

When Nico left, the terror shifted completely to my brother-in-law, calling and cycling all day passed his house, his windows were smashed at night and the company car set on fire, my brother-in-law only went out into the street armed, he called me to do the accounting, I wasn't flabbergasted going to his house after what had happened, so instead of driving to his house with my car, I walked through Nieuwmarkt and via an alley under / past an old people's home that ended up in the Keizerstraat, his street at a children's playground, so I could keep my eyes open, the closer I got to his house the more vigilant I got, once at his door the nerves really screamed threw my throat, if I could turn my head 360 degrees I would have done it, that psychopath clearly freaked me out, once in front of the door I saw indeed that his windows were boarded up, I called ... *WHO!* ?? I hear my brother-in-law yelling, me *bro, open up!.* I heard him opening several locks before the door opened. He gestured with one hand that I had to come in quickly, once inside he quickly looked out at both sides when I saw that he had a firearm in his hand behind his back, the tempers were getting heated, that was very clear.

For a man "who was under attack" he was quite calm, we did the bookkeeping, although not as accurate as usual, once finished he says, *"come i want to show you something"* then we walked to his garage, which was more of a small warehouse, by city center standards, a piece of a thing.

He opened the drawer of a toolbox and takes out 2 firearms, a Glock and a revolver. The man now had a collection because i knew he also had a Berretta. *look* he says, and puts on a double shoulder holster, puts in both weapons, puts on a raincoat over it, grabs a bicycle, '*i bought this bicycle for a reason, no handbrakes*', this was a kind of grandpa bike, on the other side of the garage / shed was a large mirror with a dressed mannequin next to it, then he brings his bicycle with rear wheel up to the garage door, and says *"pay attention"*, he cycles a few meters in the direction of the mirror, steps on his rear brake and simultaneously pulls out those two cannons. click, click, they said. he drops his bike and with a grim face click, click, click, as if he were emptying the entire magazines on that mannequin, imposing, that braking and at the same time pulling those guns, and that within seconds, I praised him, and said that I was impressed and studied his jacket, because the zipper was closed to his chin, and saw that at the height of those holsters he had made two slots where he had inserted sort of mattress foam, so that he had direct access to his firearms without obstacles, he says *"I practiced this more than a 100 times, breaking,* pulling, shooting, yes I say, I noticed, in a matter of seconds, *no seconds,* he says," *in 1.2 seconds"*

He also practiced a lot at the shooting range in the west-side of Amsterdam.

He said, "*I can shoot this motherfucker between his eyes from 25 meters distance"*

I knew this had to go wrong, this is inevitable, just a matter of time.

I asked him if he had seen GG, he said that he had seen him cycle past that morning through a hole he had made in his boarded-up window where he had a view of the corner of Keizerstraat and the channel he had a plastic bag with something in it in his hand.

I also thought and vented this directly to him that I did not want to come to him anymore, and whether he wanted to do the bookkeeping in the store from now on.

I wished him the best, and very vigilantly I left his house again. Gosh, what a load fell off my shoulders once I walked into the new market among the people.

One of the following days I got a call from our manager Nico asking if I wanted to pick up a floppy and the mail from his office on the singel, this office was in the basement, in the evening I went there, parked my car on the bridge, looked very carefully around me, nothing to see, dive down stairs, try to quickly open the door, fails, bunch of keys, the wrong one, look around again, next key, after about three keys I had the right one, quickly open, in and door on inside on the hatch, turn lights on, pick up the mail and after a bit of searching I had the right floppy, turn lights off, first look through blinds to see if there was anything to see, as far as you could see from a basement, door open with the right key in my hand, close the door, ufffff, succeeded, walk to the car, start driving along the canal ... ... phone rings ... I look GG!!! Now I had ignored all his previous calls, I had to answer this one without saying anything.... *"hey my man!!! i think you forgot to locker the door from Nico!!!* and hung up, I was not even 150 meters away, I got a heart attack, that fucker had been behind me, this man gave me the creeps, without a threat nothing but just the notice, I was behind you, you could have be mine, was more than enough coming from his mouth.

A few days later around noon at home on the thorbeckeplein I got a call around noon, I saw Nico the accountant in the display,

Hey Nico I say," *it happened"*, he simply said, he said it quietly too,

 I think we all knew it would happen, still I asked *"what happened? Brother-in-law shot GG, …. when?? Really?? an hour ago, or something, in front of his door in the Keizerstraat,* me: *is he dead that GG??*

 I don't know anything mate, I only know that the whole street has been blocked and Brother in law has fled, I will keep you informed, and hangs up.

 I turned on my scanner and television, nothing was visible at the time, I got an irresistible urge to call that GG, which I did, . tuuuuuuuut… .tuuuuuuut… .his phone rang… .. an almost cheerful GG: *hey efert my man! what's wrong with your brother in law, he can't even shoot straight, Ha Ha Ha Ha!!,* and I hung up, this man is so crazy, off his skull, just got a magazine and a clip fired on him, literally heard bullets whistling around his ears, and he just laughs ?? !!! You just can't get them crazier ...

 I went to scan and turned on At 5, the local news outlet and yes, it was on the Amsterdam network At5, ") on the other side of my brother-in-law there were metro support tasks, which secured the metro, in those vans what I saw were like 4 or 5 bullet holes, even in the wall of the retirement home, and there was an interview with a shocked old poor woman, in which she said she couldn't go back to her apartment because they had to take the bullets out of the wall, it was clear from these images that GG had therefore ducked behind these vans and ran towards Nieuwmarkt, and that not one bullet had hit its target, so you see that a shooting range or a moving target, your nerves are not under control, are two completely different stories.

It is even difficult to hit a moving target with a gun or revolver from say 20 meters away, only happens in Hollywood movies, not on the street in Amsterdam, quite quickly after that the Police knew exactly who they had to deal with, Brother-in-law A.W. and GG, whose real name I did not know, never knew.

I knew where Brother in law was and called him, he was disappointed that he hadn't shot him, and I told him from last phone call that I had with GG, he told that he was working with his lawyer to turn himself in, before the police kicks the doors in from all and everyone who was dear to him, GG had meanwhile turned himself in, apparently had not fired a shot, as the investigation showed, needs no explanation that he didn't have a weapon with him either, he was on the street same day.

Brother-in-law reported himself to the police after about 5 days and was detained in Rotterdam shortly afterwards I spoke to his lawyer, and he explained that the focus of defense in court should be on tyranny of GG and the reports to the police of my brother-in-law.

Me; *reports Brother-in-law?* Yes, he went to the police station twice, after windows were smashed, and after the combo, the company car was set on fire, oh I thought, normal, vandalism insurance, building, glass or something ... and said that ...

"No, no, he said, he apparently spoke extensively about his teasing spirit, and asked, almost begged if they could do something about it, ban on the area, something, the police could not do anything, no evidence, Brother in law had made it clear that in in case it could go wrong, and he meant really wrong this is also stated in his declarations" ahhhhhh, I thought, brother-in-law had given himself a ¨carte blanche¨ ... now I know why he was the first to say to me that he was sorry he hadn't hit him, now I understood.

Lawyer went on to ask how I knew that GG, and how I knew him. *"What do you know about that man ??"* enough ... I say, *"tell me"* so I explained him ,,, ... construction, story, hells angels, ... *ok*, he says, *"do not talk about the drugs business" "logically"* i said, *"and I also call you as a witness"* afterwards I visited my brother-in-law in the jail in Rotterdam, mostly talked about the upcoming case, he also told me he had confidence in a good ending.

After about 4 to 5 months my brother-in-law had to appear in court, I was there, had meanwhile made a statement to the examining magistrate, Nico our accountant too, and the lawyer had also summoned the two policemen as witnesses, furthermore he had a printout of the telecom company, and he had managed to get a baptismal lot from that GG, if the man was really a Rambo as we thought yes or no, he turned out to have been with the special forces, and the unit he was part of were indeed lunatics, they all had some form of PTSD, which explained a lot, because there was something wrong with this man, that was 100%, that fearlessness came from somewhere.

The man was an ex-navy seal and had been repeatedly sent on missions behind enemy lines.

A man who had seen much death and destruction, that was certain. Printout from telecom company showed that my brother-in-law had been called more than 800 times by GG, and not the other way around, the statement from me and Nico's, the reports, and the statements of both police officers, which normally do not help you much, on the contrary, but in this case they worked out well. In a few days he was released, and even received compensation!!! brother-in-law had given himself carte blanche, had he shot him that day, had he walked away with it, 100% Also, that GG got a ban, which meant he had to move, and we contacted the owner and threw a bucket of shit around about that GG, that he sold crack from the property, hid weapons, and that we knew from "reliable sources". had heard that he was a pedophile.

That jungle drum worked well, the building was empty in no time, soon after he was gone, to where we do not know, but I did hear that he died of a heart attack several years later the Devil rest his soul, Amen

[Though i even went to the National library in Den Hague to look for news paper articles, i couldn't find anything back about the shooting]

"Pumpkin head"

My brother-in-law was quite a different man after his detention, a bit timid, and still on his guard, I knew if he wearies specific jackets that he was armed, furthermore it remained calm with guys from motorcycle club, of course it helps when people know that you are armed, and also that you are willing to use it, which my brother-in-law had showed, though without result, but still, he tapped the specific boxes twice, he had them, and used them, this helps no doubt about it.

Still, after some bullshit with RIP Tony M from the club on the terrace, brother-in-law was done with it, he wanted something different, he wanted to sell the whole lot, he said that slowly but surely the coffee shops in Amsterdam would be over and throughout NL, it became clear from the media that within political circles who were lobbying so coffee shops could no longer sell hash and alcohol together, so a choice had to be made, the licensing system would be adjusted, and coffee shops closer than 500 meters from a school had to close their doors. All this did not bode well. He wanted to sell me Ricks for 425,000.guilders which I could afford in itself, but due his own prognosis about the future of coffee shops in NL and the incident with Tony M. {which I had more to do with than he did} because Tony M had indicated *"that whoever would take over the joint, would pay, period"* he literally said, all this made me decide to refrain, Ide had taken all the currents out of the porridge, both with regard to suppliers and customers.

I didn't feel like all those headaches, the store was eventually sold to a Frenchman, Joel, who had a clothing store 50 meters away. And a restaurant nearby, The Hunter's Bar which was by the way named after my brother-in-law's Rottweiler Hunter and of which there are now more than 20 coffee shops in Holland with the same name went to Nico the accountant, what happened with the greenhouse effect I don't know but it's now a concern that exists of a variety of coffee shops and a Hotel. My brother-in-law put all his money into a bagel bakery, when no one had even heard of bagels, I myself also put 50,000 hfl in his bagel adventure, I think man with foresight, Jewish, all his money in those bagels, that must be sound, it later turned out that I was wrong, money gone, and the bond I had with my brother-in-law also.

Joel, the new owner, wanted me to supply the store. In fact, something I had been doing for the past 6 years, only I had to advance the stuff and that amounted to 25,000 guilders out my pocket, after some insistence I agreed. He was a bit of an character, the man had a pony tail, and his hair slicked back with a pot of gel or something, usually wore a black leather jacket, and black cowboy boots , had a very deep, heavy, cracking voice, and spoke English with a heavy French punch to it, when I went to his house for the first time I saw really what kind of dude he was, I noticed in his bathrobe that despite the man was not fat, he retained a lot of moisture, not only his head looked like a pumpkin, but there was totally no definition in his body, not surprisingly I noticed during my visit, came at the door at 12 o'clock and could see that the man had just woken up, he would take a shower and if I wanted to wait on the sofa in the meantime his wife Ruth gave me a coffee, well that just jumping in the shower took like 25 minutes, once finished he led me to his office, that's where he puts his espresso on his desk, then he opened a bottle off Perneaux, filled a glass and opened up a draw where he took out.....yes, a bag off cocaine, " you want"? He asks   I looked at my Audemars piguet watch

" bit to early mate" he makes two big lines, drinks his espresso in mean time, than shufs the 2 lines up his nostrils, drunk the shot off Perneaux, than he lights his Gauloise cigarette, " i am ready when you are" he says, not a pretty spectacle all in all when you are just awake, no wonder that he retained a few gallons off moisture left and right around his body.

But because I financed everything i was stuck with this dude, and what he does with his body he must know for himself, but don't like it when people make me wait while they shower, no respect in my eyes, I was so busy that in the meantime I had asked for help from a "friend" nicknamed mr. Handsome his business at that time were slot machines and he was the son of a well-known Dutch boxer, his father Ruud K. won the European champion light heavy weight in 1982 and defended his title ten times

 I didn't get along with that Joel, so i had the work passed onto handsome , but soon i noticed there was also little cohesion between Joel and handsome, apparently there was a lot of mistrust on the part of Joel, because he always thought our products were too expensive, and he had friends who could get so-and-so cheaper, so when the store had a good turnover that week I calculated that if I put all that week's money in my pocket we would be almost even, I would even lost 2 a 3000 but was fed up with the man and took that for granted.

I went to his house in person to do the bookkeeping, something handsome did every week.

In one bag the turnover of the week was about twenty thousand, and in the other bag 14 empty envelopes with administration in it, and a calculation of what he still owed me in trade.

Ding dong....... pumpkin head opened with a Gauloise between his lips and said as he tightened the belt of his bathrobe, "why you? Where is handsome?? Me also with French slung, "this is why mon ami" and put the bag with the 14 empty envelopes on his dining table, and a calculation that he still owed me a small 3000 guilders, and told him that from now on he needed to contact his friends who buy everything cheaper anyway.

Also, I brought a bag with scales and a few cheese knives, his Gauloise almost fell out of his mouth in astonishment.... "Butte...Butte, You, you, cannot do this, ...

"Listen Joel, I can do what I want" *And* walked out of his door to never see him again, not long after that I heard that he died of a brain hemorrhage , ...gosh, how strange is that, I thought

"DIGAF"

In the meantime I had found another very lucrative source of income I had come across a South African who "flipped hashish over", so material that was broken, dried out, water damaged, which was basically unsaleable he made alive, he took me into his kitchen, and i witnessed what an artist this man was, I saw bread in it immediately, and i mean 5 grains of bread with double butter on it. I bought all the water damage stuff and all the broken samples of hash that i could find, didn't matter what it was, as long as it didn't have salt water damage, bought some original products , in this case "border afghan" then the south African laid everything in his freezer, he had an industrial sausage maker machine, a monster of a thing, 4 feet wide, and a 7 feet long, weighed easy 800 pounds, once the products were frozen he smashed everything to bits, added some ghee oil (vegetal oil from Indian shop) and repeatedly processed that material threw that machine until everything was homogeneous, and he pressed it so he made exactly the product we wanted to copy, in this case border afghan, including packaging and gold stamp, market price was 2400 guilders, the south African worked for 100 guilders per kilo, I sold it for say 2250, just below market price, only nice thing was that it never cost me more than 16 to 1700, depending on material available, so you're talking about 40,000 profit on 100 kilo, people loved the stuff, just couldn't make enough of it. Passed by 3 times a week to unload trade in and out in front of the South African's door, I searched city and country for material, at a certain point it became more difficult to buy the depreciated material, it just wasn't there anymore, then I tried it with Moroccan depreciated mixing material, earned even more on it, but it's natural to imagine I couldn't make a consistent product, so customers had more and more complaints about my Romeos and Juliet's, the stamps I had on it, then i changed the stamp for a while of that of a pharaoh, then everyone suddenly wanted those pharaoh's , it was just more or less the same crap, after some time they also fell out of favor, tried various stamps. But sometimes the whole thing had to be put back in the freezer and smashed to pieces again and again in the meat grinder with an improved formula. We were now many stamps further and I was once again double parked unloading the South African door in the center of Amsterdam, quickly get boxes in his house run out again, "make something nice of it" I say to the South African as I get back in the car with honking cars behind me, he yells "what kind of stamp should i put on it?" I say "do i give a fuck"!! A few days later I pick up my trade, inspect the product, cut off a corner, bendability, and look at the stamp, DIGAF?!, I say to him, "WTF of stamp is this mate? Then he says, you really did say DoIGiveAFuck! to me. Was a real cracker! Flooded the market with DIGAFŚ, my phone was glowing red, everybody wanted them, had a good name the formula had worked well, unfortunately this one was also impossible for me to make a consistent product, and after a while because of negative feedback I left the product alone but if I had demand, say if I was called for an order, I called my suppliers if they had broken water damage stuff, if that wasn't the case, I then called the customer that a container from Pakistan was on its way, So I kept a warm relationship with the customer, and I didn't have anything in stock that might remain unsold because of the inferior quality, or worse I had to have it pressed again for even more money and effort. Only the South African had a problem, a problem that I would also have to deal with in later years, he could sometimes not be reached for days, prostitutes and drugs, had to drag him out of the Amstel hotel once, because my trade had been with him for days, and i had a customer who called me crazy, this was not the first time he had put me in such a situation, so I decided to continue myself, same set up, a big Wolff sausage machine one that went on 380 volts, I remember It had 4 hp, that seems to be a lot, rented space and put air conditioning in it, because it gets very hot from all that friction of the material, big freezer and we were ready for action, I started imitating a higher segment, in this case blocks of 3.5 and 4.5 kg, they called it power afghan. Buy the original material, add water damage and chunks of old stuff, put it in the freezer, so much percent of this, so much of that, through the machine, put it in thick plastic, press, shape, cellophane jacket around it, sticker on it, done! What a hit, especially a dude called Aart, a boy from Dordrecht who lived near the Okura hotel called me nuts about this product, my phone didn't stop, the man was sometimes in such a hurry to get those blocks obtained that if the material hadn't even cooled down yet I had to deliver, than of course when he inspected them "hey, those things are all warm", "yes Aart, you're in such a hurry mate , we just got those things out of the truck, are hidden not far from the engine block", Aart had a cafe on the Zeedyk, one of the roughest streets in those days, and not long after fell dead from his balcony hotel in Thailand, his girlfriend, a solidly built woman certainly compared fragile Aart has been imprisoned for a while, man lay too far from the facade, it had to be found out whether it was a thump or push story. [Could have been a push story because they were always fighting]

"Missing envelop"

The pressing went on for some time, money came in with buckets, until too many copycats appeared on the scene, then gains got smaller, so the fun too. I did a lot of business with one so-called hash office at that time, most of them well-organized organizations and there were quite a few around. Groups that focused on brokering, so say bought from importers, mostly on credit, pierced that trade to coffee shops and traders who and to people who had foreign contacts again, usually the people in such a group had the same name, the Nico's, Franssen de Joopen or the Johnny's, I had been doing business with one in particular for many years, the leading figure was a certain Cees H., a character, besides he loved smoking spliffs all day but also very passionate about the business.

To give you an idea of what amounts were earned, I bought approximately 80% of trade i needed from his organization, these were delivered and because the trade went so fast, this went all on credit and I paid every Friday afternoon while enjoying a glass of high end white wine called Chassagne

Montrachet or something of that class, I had complete confidence in their accounting, was "state of the art" for that time, amounts ran into the hundreds to sometimes more than a million a week. I once I had to pay an amount of around 7 hundred thousand, I paid this as usual end of every week, but once there i thought there was little left, I also vented this by saying something like "Gosh I spent a lot last week" Cees showed me my printout and said it was really what it was. No further discussion that afternoon, on Monday afternoon one of the employees of the organization passed by our shop and asked if I wanted to visit the office in the heart of the city center that afternoon, I said "*but it's not Friday yet",..*" *just pass by apparently it is important ",* he said, so I went to the office at the end of the afternoon, rung bell, waving at cameras and the heavily secured door opened, Cees himself welcomed me, "hey boy" he said completely delighted, walked to their desk and the bottles of exclusive wine and glasses were on the table I say "gosh, is it someone's birthday or something?" …"Yes yours!" He said ". I sit down and he fills a glass with a big smile on his face, he looks at me and says, "don't you miss anything?" " No, why?" I say Then he slides a closed envelope to me, "yours", I open it and in it a very thick pile of 1000 guilder notes, hundred and seven to be exact, "we had a problem last Friday", he says "accounting had too much cash left we broke our heads on it, but since you said you had spent a lot last week and then we delved a little more into your accounting, we figured it had to be yours" " oh ok, that's always nice" and after I gave my thanks we all went on with our day, as if it was nothing. Mind you 107,000 guilders around 1997 was worth the same, if not more than 107,000 euros now. We earned enough and we were honest with each other. That was the fact of the matter.

Because the cooperation was so good with them, Cees offered me to merge with their organization, organization had storage depots "stash houses" couriers, a lifelike meeting room, everything with the latest gadgets, everyone had a handheld HP computer with encryption, headquarters was equipped with computers with the latest encryption technology The intention was to open a new office for me, I would get a percentage of not only my office but profit of the entire organization.

I agreed and we found a location for a new office on the Stadhouderskade. But I had to show the back of my tongue concerning my contacts, all my customers and suppliers and my pressing shop had to integrate into the organization.

With every tap I would get 12.5%, a tap was 1 million net profit, the organization turned 4 or 5 taps a year, I actually went down in income, but could now go on holiday and my percentage continued, we also worked during office hours, also worth something.

Cees ran the whole thing like a real company, with charts, statistics, and meetings every week. He even had investors who he gave returns on shares that he issued. There was one "misery" about the man, I was a champion spending money, but this man had invented it. Before our office had earned 1 guilder, we were about 100 k behind, new facade, complete renovation including hidden secret compartments and doors.

The man also had countless employees, one for the encryption, technical service, cleaning women, sandwich bakers, bicycle repair men, window cleaners, motivators, etc.

All mountains of expenses, to make a tap net (million) you had to earn two, then he kicked out some framework figures left and right and confiscated their percentages so that at a certain moment he took half of the tap and me 12.5%, cooperation lasted top 2 years, good luck and bye bye

My life didn't change much after stopping the cooperation with Cees. I flogged merchandise all over Europe, had about 500 k of working capital, customers in France, Scandinavia, Italy, Germany. Got to know some serious Moroccan operators because, they knew the game, the mocro's we called them in Holland There were fewer and fewer Dutch operators. It was mainly Abdul A. Abdul K de B, and Abdel C. Didn't need any more Dutch to bring it from A to B. Also continued to serve Dutch local customers, less money in it but apparently, I thought it was cool or something to show that I could arrange everything. Later on, that was a big mistake on my part. I had taken all the currants out of the porridge after my brother-in-law, but should have focused on the very thick currants, not the dried out little ones. Then came another problem. Got paid in all kinds of currencies, French Franc, Crowns, Deutsch Mark, Sterling, etc. This became increasingly difficult with the new MOT act. You could completely forget the official change offices, but there were several Egyptians who still exchanged large amounts in an alley behind, Madame Tussaud But bad exchange rates and bills often didn't add up. So unbelievably, through a manager of the BEXO (border exchange office) of the Central Station, I obtained an address in Antwerp in the well-known Diamond neighborhood Pelikaanstraat to be precise, so I took the plunge and went to Pelikaanstraat. Corluy was the name of that office. Hard to find, many jewelers, other exchange offices too. After some searching, I found it. Shabby door with bell with camera and buzzer. Door opened. I went upstairs, armored door, buzzer again and then I entered a dark shabby waiting room. Especially that armored door and the shabbiness appealed me. There was a big fat guy with a blouse, chest hair and a gold chain around his neck. Kind of sopranos type. Shook my hand firmly with a real Antwerp accent: Please come along. Door secured again, knocks on door, waves to camera, buzzer, door open. There was another guy counting on one of those printing calculators and there was, as I saw, a few hundred k of change on the table against the wall. Allee, what can i help you with. I told him that I occasionally received large sums of money from a boat dealer, but that this was impossible to exchange in the Netherlands. He said, in that case you have come to the right place. You can walk in here without notice up to about 20 million Frances. Above that, you must call the day before. 20 million francs is approximately 1.1 million guilders in them days exchange rate equivalent of about 400.000 £

Rates were also very attractive. Much better than with the Egyptians of Tussaud So after that I regularly went to Antwerp with my new Volvo T5 R with a few hundred thousand in change

Earned not only on merchandise but also on the exchange. On a few 100 k around 3%. So, driving to Antwerp yielded easy 6000 guilders. Amounts increased, sometimes 7 to 8 hundred thousand guilders. Then it became known that I had a good address to switch currencies. Soon after S. and R. an homosexual guy who everyone knew as the poofter came to visit me.

We're stuck with 600,000 pounds. As usual with sterling in 5, 10, 20 and 50 denominations. Then you are talking about 2 large travel suitcases full. Another big mistake I made. Did not even use money from own customers, but went with money from others, purely to exchange. Had calculated that I would earn about 19,000 guilders on it. But still, Ronald de Poofter said:

"You know who you arrange this money with, don't you? This money belongs to Curtis W. He's not going to like this when it's gone"

I had heard of him. A well-known criminal from Liverpool who lived in the Netherlands at the time and after all this spend most of his life in prison. I say to him: *man... 'no 'worries, 'i 'already 'exchanged millions so it will be fine.* Agreed with handsome that we would split the risk by dividing it into 2 suitcases and traveling independently.

And I called S. and Ronald de P. so that they could bring the sterling. Of course, they wanted it back in guilders. That Sterling was somewhere around 2.80 back then. So, these were 1.6 million hard guilders

Called Corluy that I would pass by the next day and that the amount is above 20 million. Francs. 'Allee, *how much you have?* he said. I told him about 30 million. Counting all night with 1 money counting machine. Until the machine was smoking so to say, bundling everything and elastics around it was only ready around 6 o'clock in the morning. In the end, a few hundred sterling were short, apparently there were a few counterfeit notes because the machine did not count them. *Hurry up...* I said to handsome! And told him that we would keep a distance of 15 to 20 km. We would conform to this by calling every 20 minutes. Everything went perfectly. Until I drove into Antwerp. Got stuck near the target location. Behind a moving truck and eventually too late. Stressed out, I drove into the street that runs parallel to Pelikaanstraat. And who do I see driving there in front of me? Hand some's golf VR6! Other than that, there was no parking space. Driving laps. In the meantime, call handsome

"This was precisely not the intention, mate! He replies 'there *is not much I can do about it, I mean half hour driving around with a little million in the trunk is not the solution or what?* ..my reply *"don't matter anymore mate we park together"* Strangely enough when I drove through that parallel road again, two men in a Passat made a gesture that I could park in their place. I wasn't suspicious, drove slowly, looked for a place and just as I drove past, he turned on his turn signal and reached out. The perfect place, right at the head of the Pelikaanstraat! I took the large travel case out of my Volvo and waited for handsome. After some time, he arrived with exactly the same suitcase. We entered the Pelikaanstraat, which is closed to motorized traffic. About 150 meters before I got to Corluy I suddenly got taken by surprise and laid on the ground with the barrel of a pistol in my cheek and a bunch of angry looking men above me, and this all within a second. It happened so fast that I barely realized what was going on. Also saw Mr. handsome lying on the floor. Then the shackles were put on. Pffff we

were certainly not ripped. I was placed right in the back of the Passat, which had just made way for my Volvo.

Shit I thought... those Corluy's will be observed   Mr. handsome went separately in another car in the back. Here we went ... I saw the suitcases being loaded into a third car. At least 8 men were involved in the operation. Once at the desk I was heard after an hour by Commissioner Janssen and a Flemish flaming detective. Belgians are very polite in their social approach. Good day he says. Can you explain where and from whom that money comes from? I said the money is legitimate and that handsome knew nothing about it. He only helped me. I didn't want to declare anything else and told him I wanted a lawyer. He says: We are currently counting the money and asked me how much it was. I told him, except for a few hundred pounds, exactly 600,000 pounds. I was taken to the police cell again and thought they must be busy with that Mr. handsome now. The next day we were brought to trial, and both placed in custody. To the Begijnenstraat. A very old 18th century prison in the center of Antwerp. Hand over all your personal things, including your clothes because I don't know now, but then you had to put on a grey prison suit. Was put in all restrictions, but compared to the Netherlands, that means nothing. Because I could just talk to a cleaner who happened to be a dude from Rotterdam who was also in for money laundering. Asked through the hatch if he didn't know a good lawyer. Vercraeye, Joris, that's mine. I'll call for you. That talk went little by little because there was a red, black sign in front of my door: RESTRICTIONS. So, he lingered in front of my door while he was mopping, and he promised to call that attorney as soon as possible. Of course, there was also talk about what I was in for. He told me, there are 2 Dutch people walking around here for the same thing. *How much"* he asked I say *1.6 million converted.*

Waaaaaa fuck! In Rotterdam dialect.

And continues *me for 260000 guilders.* Me again: *How long have you been inside? Almost 7 months*, he says. Oellalaaa, I thought. This may take some time. The next day after walking in a cage for an hour with a prison suit that was far too small, I was called up. Sir S.? Yes, I say .. Attorney for you. Now you must take off your grey coat first and you get a white coat. So, they can recognize that you are going to your lawyer. I walked into a hallway with glass doors on both sides. Busy, lots of shouting. I am looking for a man who sits alone. Of course, I don't know what he looks like, that attorney. Walk back and forth. Of about 30 doors, I see 2 people sitting alone. Open the door at first and say: *Vercraeye.* Yes, he nods. *Mr. S. I can't do much for you right now. The file is still classified. All I know is that you are charged with a good 100 million money laundering charges.*

Huh? I say to him, *that's not possible.   1.6 million is something like 30 million francs!*

No, he says. *Apparently, they were on top of you for a long time.   "Are those Soprano-like Corluy's inside too?"*
"No As far as I know, only you and your friend.   And continues:" I fear those Corluy's.   are a front or have a covenant with the police."

Vercraeye told me his wages and I agreed. He would represent me. At the end of the same day, after dinner, two sjefkes, as prison guards in Belgium are called, opened my door. *"Lawyer for you*," he says. I say he must be wrong because I just saw mine. He checks the list and then checks my door number. No, he says. *"Really for you Are you coming with us?* Well, let's go. Putting on such a much too small canvas jacket again and they led me down the hall, through some of those automatic click doors and back to that lawyer visiting quarters that looked very modern and light compared to the rest of this complex. What an old, dark, depressing mess it was. I walked in, was not a human being to be seen very quiet

No prisoner, no lawyers except one. At the very end. Actually, the door you looked straight at. Walk past doors, look at both sides, I'm half past.... Nothing ..Take another look at that man at the end of the hall. I think damn... I know him, right? That's Moskowitz. The moment I look at him he makes a waving motion at me. Like, ...Yes, I am the one.

(Max Moskowitz is a very well-known lawyer in Holland after he defended the Heineken kidnappers, he had more of a celebrity status and was often a guest on talk shows)

Man took a good look at me first. Looks at a paper / file with reading glasses. Calls my name. *Mr. S. That's you I suppose*, I nod. He says *I got sent by Mr. Willem Vos.* I knew that one. That's the owner of HAG.

A company that provided our bars of automatic system for beer and shots, . Whether I wanted to use his services. 15,000 in advance and another 10,000 when trial is there. PFFFFF, I say *Mr. Moskowitz. I just lost 1.6 million. I have just transferred 100,000 francs to a Belgian lawyer. And now this one on top? Who is that Belgian lawyer if I may ask?* He asked with by the way always a soft monotone voice. *Vercraeye*, I say. *Never heard of him,* he says.

And continues. *Mr. S. I have a license to act as a lawyer in*

Belgium. You know me. You know, I've defended and gotten out much bigger crooks than you. I know all the prosecutors and judges here. You are entitled and deserve a good defense and that's exactly what I can guarantee.

He says: "*I see you are having a hard time*"

I reply to *Mr. Moskowitz. "I am not concerned about the 15000". No, no,* he interrupts me. *I mean, sitting here, the circumstances ... I'll show you something.* Unties one of his cufflinks, rolls up his sleeve and reveals a tattooed number.

Mr. S. I got this tattooed as a little boy in Auschwitz. And I sat there until I was 14. This is a banquet hall compared to where I've been. I have to say, I was impressed, I lent back and said it's *okay. I arrange that you will receive your 15,000.* "*But you will have to do it together with that Belgian*"

"*that's no problem two know more than one furthermore, you will not see me much. I'm not a social attorney, so to say I sometimes come here in Antwerp to eat kosher and i have two further clients here.* He wished me strength and left.

And because of what he said I felt like I was walking back to my cell on a cloud. I am thinking what a dick I was. This was really a holiday park compared to Auschwitz. After a week or so of limitations, I was taken for questioning. 2 sleuths wanted additional explanations and I had no idea what the handsome one had declared. But I once told Corluy that the money came from a boat dealer. I think I'll stick with that. Once inside, always that friendly hello with the soft G. *Mr. S. Can you explain, as he puts a list in front of me, where the money from these transactions comes from?* I think, shit. From the first transaction to the last transaction, and it contains still images from cameras that were hanging in the change office. And the last transaction was not £ 600,000 but £ 534,410. *'In your first statement, you said it was £ 600,000'*

I say .. *look with such a machine sometimes a note is not accepted, so it could be that here and there a note is missing. But then you are talking about 1000 to 2000 at the most, not 65000. I say someone has had long fingers.* This statement is, of course, distorted. This is apparently brought up at the police schools internationally. In the end it stated something like: The suspect admits that he counted it lazily. This gives even more the suspicion that the money comes from illegal activities. I also issued a statement from whom the money came, and I had once met a Canadian who was in the boat trade. A guy who lived somewhere in a fancy apartment near Vondelpark. I knew exactly where he lived but I didn't know this for those sleuths. I described him exactly as I knew him and his name was Andrew Southall or Suttle and he lived in the door on the left, so and so and on the bottom one, but of course he had fuck all to do with it.

© Eric Lalmand (Belga)

Begijnenstreet jail In heart center Antwerp

And he says: *and all of this money did you receive from this one man? Yes, I say.* He again: *all transactions? Yes, exactly* I say... Then suddenly he pulled an ace out of his sleeve. A crumpled piece of paper which I recognized from my bookkeeping. On which so many kilos of this and that stood for so much etc. Was only a part.

Apparently, something I had torn apart and thrown out the window.

I looked closely at a copy, and I exaggerated completely: *how did you get that??? Found under your seat,* he says with a smile on his face. F#$%k sake I thought ... must have blown back by the wind. And I say I don't know about it; I often lend my car. So .. Then they came up with another beautiful one. A bank deposit in a Luxembourg bank in my name. From 50,000 guilders. Found in your companion's car he says Tjesusss. I did tell him multiple times to leave it with his mother or mother-in-law. He had been driving around with it for weeks. I knew then that I could say goodbye to all this money. I had already had extensive talks with lawyer Vercraeye, and he had already said that it would be a very difficult story to any of this money back.

All we had to go for is to keep my detention as short as possible by offering bail. Both cars had also been seized, but they were both on a lease contract with a well-known company in Rotterdam. Handsome later turned out to have stated, as I had stated from day 1, that he had simply been asked to drive a suitcase for me to Antwerp and had never been to Corluy. So, they had little or nothing against him. He was on the street in like 5 or 6 weeks. I had to stay in this luxury hotel a bit longer, Life in the medieval dungeons on Begijnenstraat number 2 was not easy. There were zero activities. I remember asking a sjefke during time out if there were sports activities or a gym. Then he pointed to a concrete ping-pong table on the yard There was really nothing. Simply inside 23 hours a day and shower together 3 times a week. And cinema once a week. Of course, I went there. There I met some Dutch people. Also, one from the Hague. He also turned out to have Max Moskowitz as a lawyer. First thing he said: *did he show you his camp tattoo too?* Yes, I say .. he again. *He does that to everyone hahahaha.* I was a bit disappointed. The frills say the pencil was off at that moment. Had met a Belgian during airing in the yard. Didn't look like some type of delinquent or junkie. Well groomed guy with all his teeth, a baby face and expensive Versace shoes. I was still alone in a cell. He at that moment also, but most of the time with a junkie. He warned me that they could just as easily put a junkie in my cell and suggested we start lofting together. I agreed, he sat for large-scale VAT fraud. Had been in custody for more than 20 months, for 100ths millions of francs, so tens of millions of guilders. Once I entered his cell, I saw from the pictures on the wall that the man did indeed have a high life. Photos of Ferrari, Mercedes, and a massive villa and photos of an attractive woman with a young child. *"that's my wife and child"* he says and gives some explanation about who, what, where. Too bad for him that everything had been confiscated except wife and child.

In the meantime, something else happened that put a lot of extra pressure on me, late in the evening my cell door was opened and a chefke brought my private clothes, with the announcement that I would be lifted early in the morning to be taken to the border to be heard by detectives from the Amsterdam corps of the group "serious crimes", I immediately... .*but but for what ?!* .. *"No idea, get ready at 7.30"* I literally didn't sleep a wink that night, I mean serious crime group generally only do murder cases, so what the fuck could that be? At that time, I knew several friends who had been murdered, but they were all solved, ... mmm...except one. I had nothing to do with it, phew, everything played through my mind ... in the morning I got brought by 2 Belgian plainclothes officers to a roadside restaurant just across the border, there to meet 2 "friendly" detectives from the Amsterdam police force with my handcuffs on with a coat over it, *hello Mr. S. We want to hear from you in connection with the murder of your neighbor.*

. neighbor?

Yes, you live on Nieuwendijk 107 second floor, right? Under you lived a lady of Surinamese descent who is dead, murdered, in fact laid dead for months until she was found, she was mummified,

One of the detectives said laughing that the mice ran through her skull, windows were wide open and she was there like that for 5 months, in the context of neighborhood research they had to hear all neighbors, as I was registered there so it was my turn, Pffff, gosh a load fell off my shoulders, I told them I hadn't lived there for a long time, and had rented this out to a Canadian, and that it was a strange woman with (what I had once discovered) a large altar in her house. I had no contact with her, nothing, knew there came an old grey guy over the floor every now and then .. signed a statement and ready, all that stress for a downstairs crazy woman, and now a dead crazy person, by the way, heard much later that the grey man in question say her boyfriend has been convicted of either manslaughter or murder of her. Later talked to Dan the M. to whom I had passed my apartment on and asked if he had never heard anything, the police had interviewed him too, and he had noticed the foul smell when he went down by her door, but thought that she had left her garbage bags in her hallway, all the more because she had said she would go to Suriname the last time he spoke to her, so those garbage bags were the lady herself. Months passed and I had never seen Moskowitz again. Vercraeye had been a regular and hinted that he was not too happy with Moskowitz's collaboration. He consulted with him a few times about the strategy, but he got the idea that Moskowitz had no file knowledge at all. Pffff. I thought.... Did I pay 25,000 for that? The case was due to be dealt with pro forma shortly after and Vercraeye promised to do his best. The day had arrived. The day before my private clothing was brought and early in the morning I was lifted with handcuffs and put in a (was winter) ice-cold Hanomag bus where there was room for about 20 inmates. One of my handcuffs was released and attached to a steel pipe. And there I sat with my arm up in an ice-cold van for at least 1 hour before we left. At the court I was put in a dungeon, dark musty cell with shit smeared on the walls.

Max Moskowitz surrounded by his sons, all lawyers

Eventually brought into the courtroom, had to sit on a bench, in front of me 3 judges, behind me Vercraeye and Moskowitz, on the left the prosecutor. The prosecutor came first and read the charges. According to him, I was an indispensable link in a criminal mafia-like organization with the aim of laundering criminal money. And mentioned the amount of 100 + million Belgian francs. And that I also knew that this was criminal money and that I therefore also drove a lease car. Also, my statement that the money belonged to one Andrew Southall was pure nonsense. And of course, with the piece of accounting found from under my seat, then something that felt like a slap in the face, the prosecutor showed the enlarged piece on a big screen and read exactly what it said, painful I must say. It was now Vercraeye's turn. This one went more on the technical evidence. He said our client has provided a detailed statement from whom the money came. The piece of paper found was printed and dated from months ago, even far before the first transaction in Antwerp. The car was not a rental car, was on a purchase lease contract and was already 80% paid by me. In the meantime, I hear Moskowitz flipping through the newspapers. I look around and yes, he has a stack of newspapers in front of him and I see him frantically leafing through them. I thought to myself, isn't it unbelievable for those 25 grands? Is he looking for ads or something? Vercraeye continues to cackle, Moskowitz to leaf through. And yes, at one time he says: excuses confrere, may I interrupt you for a moment? And apologizes to the judges too. Meanwhile, fold a newspaper into a fold and continues; "Members of the court, now we have all heard the prosecutor say that our client's statement is pure nonsense" Then I would like to draw your attention to the following: I have this morning's Telegraph in my hand. There is an article with a headline here" which i read out loud, Collaboration between the Belgian and Dutch police lacks in money laundering quote: Commissioner Janssen, who also led the case against our client, complains that he receives little or no cooperation from the Dutch police about the origins of the money which in almost all cases are leading back to the Netherlands like this they couldn't determine who the real owners were from the confiscated money Period, says Moskowitz and now the key question he says: how can the prosecutor say that what our client says is nonsense? He says to the judges: Will you allow me to give the newspaper to you? He hands the to the court clerk and says with a smile, you can keep It. I see all 3 judges with furrowed eyebrows looking at the article with great interest.

PHENOMENAL!!, or what they call in Jewish mazel tov. This man probably hadn't read a letter in my file and is pulling four aces and a joker out his sleeve. The judges muttered and asked if Vercraeye would add anything. No, said the somewhat surprised Vercraeye. Then 1 of the judges said: then we will withdraw to debate, and we will answer today about a bail. I went back into the dungeon and a few hours later that medieval gate was opened. That jailer: lawyer for you. He leads me to the attorney' visiting room and I see Vercraeye with a smile. You have bail! 1 million francs. In guilders 56000. But you must arrange it within 24 hours otherwise they can withdraw it. Sure, I say. Cash good? No problem, he says. Next day I walked out of Begijnenstraat number 2. Back in Amsterdam it was soon business as usual again. Can remember just before i got arrested a dated a girl Deborah, a girl who worked across the canal in a coffee shop. I had just been to New York with her before I was arrested and slept in the famous Waldorf Astoria hotel. She first saw me after I had been released for weeks. Gosh she says: I hear you fly all over the city, but you don't have a minute for me? You're even busier as a

{Not one of the confiscated £600,000 has ever been recovered, nor have I ever seen the 50,000 guilders I had parked in the Luxembourg bank, and I don't need to explain the one million Belgian francs I paid as bail never came back either, I never went to the trail and I got sentenced to 18 months after that I stayed away for 10 years until the case expired, so the trip to Antwerp cost a total of almost two million old-fashioned hard Dutch guilders, keep in mind that this was in the time when you still bought a three-room house for 100,000 guilder}

A few years later I paid a total of almost 700.000 back to R the poufter and S, this because they said they couldn't retrieve the money in relation to the find of the piece of accounting under my seat, if this money ended up at Curtis W. I don't know)

Belgium popular for money laundering black money

More than half of the cases come from the Netherlands

2 minutes reading time   ✎ Turn off hatching

BRUSSELS - Nearly half of the money laundering operations in Belgium that were discovered in the first half of this year come from the Netherlands. This appears from the official data of the Belgian Reporting Center for Unused Transactions (CEL).

This Hotline qualified 62 transactions as "illegal" in the first six months of this year; Dutch people were involved in 29 cases and 25 transactions came from Belgians. Antwerp is at the top of the list of money laundering operations, followed by Brussels and Ghent.

The Belgian Hotline receives more money laundering reports from Flemish banks than from Walloon banks. The detection of suspicious transactions is different in Belgium than in the Netherlands, where the banks test transact against a number of established criteria. If

__"He that walk with the wise shall be wise."__.

In the early 90s I moved from the heart of the center to the Old West part of the city, a spacious two floor apartment with a garden, i had entered into a relationship with a lady and she was pregnant, and she had just like me a child from a previous relationship, so we had to move to something bigger, now you would think that once I left the red light district behind, house with garden, new-born on its way then the little tree and bee creature feeling will also take over, i mean like family man, responsibility, peace, but nothing was further from the truth, it was around this time i started to lose total control over my addictions.

If you pollinate your membrane every other week or so in the manner like I did, not only everything goes "tits up" on such conscious nights, but also your judgment of characters is going down the drain, in fact really your judgment about anything is pollinated. I was like a chicken without a head, its what they say " when you only put shit in, only shit will come out" spent money like water, had our new rental apartment completely renovated, everything, new kitchen, breaking walls through, garden, windows, frames, shutters, 100ths of grant I threw at it, until a buddy pointed out to me if it wasn't maybe a better idea to buy the apartment instead of making the owner of the property happy, well, I hadn't thought of that, later I bought the entire 6 floor building, not that I really wanted it a building full off tenants, but unwillingly a very good move.

After I completely refurbished it and bought the tenants out I played with the thoughts of selling it, and sometimes I was not happy with the tenants of some apartments........, so a new real estate office had just opened around the corner and drove past it one day and parked my car, went in and said, "morning i have a few apartments to sell" as if they were superfluous second hand sofas, I could have counted on my fingers even though prices had already increased fivefold over the past 10 years that this would happen again in the next 10, no , they had to go like old sofas, and no I didn't have a father figure where i looked up to, or someone who grabbed me by the ass and said "bastard, why sell?! It's done! top renovated! The stuff is almost paid off!!, if you keep this you can rake in even more money every year as the highest paying job or with a well running company and for both you must work! this just continues while you sleep!,

No, it had to go, wanted to "go ahead", something else, just like my mates, renovate, sell, what I didn't understand is that I had no business acumen at all, all I had was time, after all I was still young, for everybody without patience and never heard of this wise saying from Aristotle "Patience is bitter, but its fruit is sweet." Other than not taking my addiction seriously, absolutely the biggest mistake of my life.

After I sold most of the 10 floors I had in total, I bumped into a Yuri who had some "investments" and either he is a professional scammer or just a somewhat chubby twat that carts for others, he calls himself Yehudi (Jew in Arab) and claims he is a Roma or Sinti gypsy , and he suffers from ptsd syndrome, and this syndrome he got again from his grandparents who stayed during the WW2 in Bergen Belsen or Auschwitz camps, and because of that syndrome he has been one of the most violent hooligans of Feyenoord or Ajax football clubs according to him, but most likely from the local handball association from that hole where he lived, all is possible i know now.

He walked around in worn out shoes, because you could see him shuffling all over town in his Todd's or Hogan shoes, always wearing designer clothes but usually from two or three seasons back.

Talks all day long about mega deals at first class locations but always travels second class on the train, this gypsy or Jew or whatever he calls himself has only given me half-baked stories, sold me a 2000 ft. clothing store in the center of Amsterdam which ended up in a total nightmare and has Introduced me to a variety of people among them a black lad, a certain T who had far too big front teeth compared to his face, I had him set up a company, bought rolls of denim in France and we would send them to Morocco to make jeans from these denim rolls and there we would conceal Moroccan fun cigars between the jeans , at least that was the plan, setting up a company went well, giving advances even better, purchasing denim went well until those rolls had to be exported from France to Morocco, rolls that weigh easy a few tons and were easy 12 to 15 feet long for which I also paid twenty one thousand. I had to pay seven thousand for the transport which I gave to T, next day I call him to confirm whether he had transferred it, he didn't answer the phone, not all day, ... not the next day either, I already knew there was something wrong, , then in the evening

I got a text from him " *hello, I hope you don't get mad, but the money's gone",* I call, he picks up, I say " *what do you mean money gone?"* "*I lost it with gambling",* I think i screamed so loud that i messed up his frizzy hair , then the Moroccan also seemed to be unable to arrange it at all in Morocco, it wasn't his company that was the sender, his plan was to have the pants made at the sending company, then take them back for a brief moment to have a brand name put on them, and then conceal the Moroccan fun cigars in between the pants, and then have the company that made the pants in the first place send it to Europe, well I know one thing with my decades of experience, there is not one Moroccan who will send boxes, cans, toothbrushes or toilet paper in the name of his company for someone else without checking what's in those boxes. I had to say goodbye to a total of 35,000 investments.

Mr. Roy is a different story, is of Aruban descent, very lightly bronzed, distantly Negro, a proper poufter, when I met him, he lived in a chic penthouse in a one of the better neighborhoods in Amsterdam and even had an Audi A8 with driver, his business was human resources that is chic for say employment agency

He wanted to set up a dispatch in Mongolia and needed a cash injection of 160,000, within 6 months back he said, would get back 200 for the 160   Mongolia was the fastest growing economy at that time, where China grew eight, nine or ten percent on an annual basis, Mongolia added another five percent. I flew to the capital Ulaanbaatar to view his enterprise had a flight via Moscow and then another ten-hour flight to Ulaanbaatar

Weird fellows those Mongolians, some were completely pissed on that plane, I had 2 seats to myself and when I came back from the toilet there was a Mongolian sleeping on my seats, was totally paralyzed from the booze and I could not even wake him up, the flight attendant managed to send the totally hammered Mongol away

Ulaanbaatar is a very dusty city that is constructed in communist style, large squares and many statues of communist leaders from the past, +25 degrees during the day and -15 at night, in the center there were some western-oriented restaurants and a large Irish pub with live music. I visited his company, he actually had a floor with a number of employees, some ladies sitting behind desks, he had a Mongolian dude working for him that drove him around, I, drove out of town with this particular dude and visited a Buddhist temple, and also some of those "gers", those typical round tents made of hides where Mongols used to live in, i dressed up as djengis khan and had my picture taken,

Then I went with Roy to a local restaurant where the specialty was all animal intestines, liver, kidneys, brains, fried, chopped, marinated, you name it. what i noticed that Roy had his eye on a Mongolian waiter who worked in that restaurant, he asked me to take pictures with my Nikon camera from him and the boy together and he tried to persuade the kid to come home with him, it became clear to me that Roy wasn't just there for work, he was more say entrepreneur and a sort of sex tourist, I felt sorry for those poor Mongolian boys who had to come to terms with that Aruban liquorice bar of him.

Flew back and lent him that 160,000 when he was back in his slightly too kitsch-decorated penthouse.

Weeks turned into months, months turned into even more months, heard little more from Roy, term had almost passed, on a rainy winter day I drive on a traffic artery in Amsterdam slowly between other cars from traffic light to traffic light, my attention goes to a guy on a bike somewhere in front of me who is fighting the elements, what stood out is that he had a huge blow in his rear wheel, hood over his head against the rain and wind, looked like torture, i almost felt pity for the dude.

Traffic picked up again so at one point came driving alongside at the same snail's pace as the dude on the bicycle and took a closer look at the man, I noticed he was wearing expensive moncler shoes, and a stone island jacket. Only then did I look at the man's face, FFs that's Roy!!!   Need little explanation if I ever got my money or not. Of course, all kinds of half-baked stories, none of which can be verified, he has paid me back something over the years, but that is not yet enough for the interest. I did hear rumors that he was kicked out of Mongolia because of his homosexual activities, could be because Mongolia is in that aspect easy fifty years behind compared to Holland. That is why Roy has to submit to financial controls to this day, how does he live, does he have a car, and if so, what kind of car, bank account so on, and keep in mind I've got a whole list of Roy's

Therefore, if you decide to lend someone money, ask for collateral, confiscate something, car, house, bicycle, birdcage, clean underwear, anything that covers the value of what you lend, otherwise you go crying and or go to war.

"Grey wolf"

I've known Atilla O from the early 90s, 2 buildings away from where I lived there was a Turkish coffee house where his father was more or less part of the furniture, at that time he had long hair and rode the bicycle of the moment, a Kawasaki ZZR, this was the Atilla in the making, have seen the most fearless man, that GG, the nastiest people, but Atilla was the man with the biggest balls, I recognized it, what was in the news papers when the police told him that he was on a kill list, without telling as usual who his kill list he was on, according to the same newspapers he seems to have said "certainly that poufter Holleeder" {Holleeder was one of the kidnappers of beer producer Heineken, and one of the most feared men in the underworld at the time} I knew him that he still lived on 3th floor in the Jordan and his son Baris was still in kindergarten.

Everyone also knows from the newspapers that his son was shot dead at the age of 26. There was also an assassination attempt on Atilla himself which made him hop a little and he had a little finger that no longer served because a bullet in his hand had blown a nerve to pieces, a strange pointy thin little finger that he could no longer bend, i joked sometime by saying to take that thing off, then people think you're a member of the yakuza club, the Japanese mafia, learn a little Japanese, add tattoos, but pinkie stuck with Atilla, he didn't fancy the idea taking it off

Atilla and I have never done business, but a lot of clubbing, white sensation including his mate Ali, he already had popping eyes of his own, and if we had all taken a lick of MDMA then you would see people all looking at Ali because he looked as if he had licked the whole bag empty, although I did not do business with Atilla, he did collect debts for me he had proved that to me once when he accompanied me in my car when we went to Haarlem to visit a mate of mine,   and just before the traffic lights he suddenly is distracted and looks obsessed at a car, we slowed down for traffic lights and he says STOP, STOP HERE NOW!, we had to stop anyway for the traffic lights, so I stopped, totally focused on that particular car on the right side in front of us he steps out, and walks straight to that car he pulls the door open on the drivers side where he pulls a guy on his jacket half out of his seat while he was in his seatbelt and starts from the get go beating the guy maniacally on his head, and I mean like 250 rpm a minute so to say, like 15 beats or so in a few seconds, he stops and yells with the face of an proper psychopath, YOU PAY YOU MOTHERF#€%^R!!! Lets go of him and walks relaxed back and steps in my car and says while pointing with his hand covered in blood to a certain direction " I know a really nice sandwich shop near by, lets go there" like nothing happened. I really laughed my balls off, I "liked" what I saw, the man was a proper psychopath, so when a certain O. owed me a 6 digit figure, because the deal was he would send some fun cigars from morocco for more than a year already and I only got stories, i asked Atilla to pay a visit to the man's butcher's shop, and after I was sure that the man was in his shop I dropped Atilla off across the street from the butcher's and I saw Atilla enter and immediately turn the open sign to closed, then he had a conversation with 2 customers in the store while the Moroccan looked in shock, after the customers had left the store, I saw Atilla go behind the counter, a moment later he left the store again- and? I ask, "Message got through" he says as he counts a pile of banknotes, *'exchanged some bullets for money'* he says , so he had emptied his clip in his cash register., made an impression because the next day an old Mercedes 200 D stopped in front of my door full of djellebas, O himself sat in the back between his uncles, he didn't get out of the car either, his father rang the doorbell and immediately started a kind of tirade about why in Gods name I could send such a lunatic to his son, while he gives me an envelope with money, i take it, and replied, "*why*"? *"For this*"! while I hold the envelope in front of his face, although not everything was in it, but it was a good start. Somewhere around 2001, Atilla wanted to buy coffee shops, he had meanwhile bought the coffee shop of Cees Houtman, who was murdered in 2005, but wanted more. He regularly asked me for advice when he came across a shop in his path, then he took accounting with him and then wanted to hear from me whether he should buy that shop or not, that is quite a responsibility with this man. So, I assisted him with advice and sometimes also with deed, I told him that a shop is worth about 1 time the annual turnover, but if this exceeds 5 times annual profit, it is too much again, you are working way too long to earn money back. The exact hashish turnover can also be manipulated, so to speak, you would have to spend a day to see what is sold in hash. He showed me a whole stack of receipts from a coffee shop in the Marnixstraat, I knew the shop and the owner, his name was V, brother of M who also had a coffee shop at the Leidse square, the shop was at a dead end in the street, I drove past it regularly and saw hardly any people inside, but based on those receipts shop turned out to have 1500 a day turnover, an average of 1000 a day, shop had to earn 280,000, I called him and said that on the basis of those vouchers that shop was interesting, with this turnover you could earn back your shop in 2 seasons. Ok, he says and thanked me kindly, he calls me a few hours later and says, " *mate, that shop is mine*", me: *have you paid yet*? *no* he says, "*you know, I am a Turk, word is word*"

A day later he calls me totally of his scull, *Arkadash*!! (Friend in Turkish) *come here!!* He told his location, a well-known sandwich shop in the Jordan where he lived 200 meters from. Enter the sandwich shop in question and see him sitting right at the window at long counter. His face looked like a thunderstorm, "*what's cooking*" I say

"*That dirty faggot sold that shop to someone else'*"

you called yesterday that you had a deal!"

"*Exactly, that stinky bastard has sold it to the slots machine man*!

afterwards?

Yes, he says, I say again, damn,

' *Did he get a better price or something?? Didn't he tell you why?* ,

"I don't give a damn mate, not a flying fuck, even if he gets a million, I had a deal for 280,000 period"

Come on he says, *"we're going there, I called him half an hour ago", he's there,* then he opens a plastic bag under the table, I look, there's a gun in it, a small type of a revolver, I look at him, and now it comes, I think depending on how you interpreted my facial expression at that moment there were 2 conclusions possible, 1 was, no mate, I don't feel like this at all, or it could also be 2, what do you want with that little shooter? It was of course the first, he says, *wait here, be right back*, well he lived around the corner, so I wait, he comes back, sits down with the same plastic bag, opens that bag discreetly under the table, he got a bloody mini Uzi or a scorpion or something like that in it!! , I think , Jesus fuck this, he says, *come on, let's go*, and walks out, once out, come on he says get in" Uffff, I thought, I say, *"go ahead my car is further on"* I made up that I had not paid the parking meter, and that I would be at the shop as soon as possible, I see him step into his BMW M5 and dash off towards the Marnixstraat that was less than a kilometer from

120

there, I leisurely walk to my car, look at my watch, hmmm, he'll be there in 3 minutes, me about 6, very calmly put on my seat belt, looking in my mirrors, as if I had my first driving lesson, turn signal on, look blind spot, there I went, 30 km per hour in a built-up area, come to the end of the street, bridge, look left and see his BMW already parked double in front of the shop, I think I'm going to find a spot to the right, parked and walk towards that shop and see the owner standing totally in shock in the doorway while the smaller Atilla with a with a very serious and passionate face is busy gesturing his story to V, he sees me coming and says, *"I'm right or wrong"?*...with what? I ask, *"with that bull shit from this faggot here of course?"* I couldn't help but agree with Atilla, I told V. *"you gave the man your word, besides I say, I don't know if you know, but the man is Turkish , and his name is on top of that Atilla,* after some talking in which V told that the slots machine man had already paid a deposit, and on top of that he had a debt with the slot machine man, did not matter to Atilla, a fine had to be paid, 100 k seemed like fair amount to him.

V the owner himself had also called a strong arm, if we would just talk to him, this strong arm arrived a little later when we were waiting outside, me and Atilla see him coming, a bald guy in a dented car, *"I know him"* I say to Atilla, he, *"me too"* as he puts his index finger to his lips, man gets out, and yes, it's the man we thought it was J. We walked away from the shop out of sight, and laughing Atilla beckons to J. to come, and J asks us, " did you guys want to buy that shop, and now create a problem? Atilla," yes" ..., then suddenly they are both all excited and laughing, like two boys who have just won a youth football tournament, J. *"Oh, well then this one is for us! we have to play this smart, and we milk him completely empty! he can give us what he receives for that shop!"* What the fine was eventually paid, i don't know, i am not aware of the further settlement

Atilla Under

Atilla Önder is one of the founders of discotheque The Sand and owner of three coffee shops in Amsterdam. He was friends with hash dealer Kees Houtman, who was liquidated in November 2005. Willem Holleeder was convicted a few years later for extorting Houtman.

Atilla's name, like that of friends like Houtman, appears frequently in police files. For example, Willem Holleeder reported to the Criminal Intelligence Unit in 2005 to say that *'he was afraid*

"Hollow doors"

Somewhere in 1999 an old client of mine contacted me who I had unfortunately introduced to my "youth mate" Frans Heinrich R. the man in question an Irish citizen, not a typical drug dealer more a bit of a student looking dude named M.

He on his turn introduced me to another Irish called Dave, or "babyface" as he got called by M.

And even though David babyface smoked one joint after the other a very active man.

David asked me if I had any contacts in South Africa to arrange a few tons of "ganja" or weed, Frans HR had of course heard that I had been there regularly and I had recently been married in Sun City (las Vegas from south Africa) I had made a trip with my then brand new wife via Mauritius and had made a tour from cape town to Pretoria, which costed me like 50 k, but that was just a "normal" amount of money when I went on holiday. But of course, during that trip i had not acquired an agenda full of contacts. I did know the Hells Angels well, of course I had contacts with the chapter in Amsterdam where I was a regular visitor to club evenings and the chapter Ijmuiden I knew some members well, but chapters Manchester and Manaus (Brazil) were also in my contact list. Because it was hard for me to say no in general, I told the Irish that I could find the right people. So, I went to a club evening, I do sing a bit of opera and once there i sang "La Dona mobile" the president Big Willem van. Boxtel liked that, a bit of PR, I asked if they could not introduce me to people in SA, either brothers in Cape Town or Johannesburg, after a few days I got the green light and a little later I flew there with Bonanza, a member of club Ijmuiden, a relaxed guy Bonanza, lived a stone's throw away from me, loves a spliff, we made it a wonderful trip and drove along the breath-taking coast of Cape Town and the surrounding area, I also met Paul, who was the vice president of the Cape Town chapter, or say not really a chapter wit capital letters compared to that of Amsterdam, more of a garage with a sign "Hells Angels" on it. The intention was to send 5 tons of weed from South Africa to Ireland, depending on the price, the question was whether he, Paul or other members of the club could not introduce me to reliable suppliers.

That was possible, but we had to travel to Pietermaritzburg near

Durban, the prices depending on the quality were between 250 and 375 converted to guilders at the time. When it became clear that the story could be filled in, I flew back to Amsterdam with Bonanza, where clear plans were made with babyface. It was him who had a paid door in Port Arlington, say customs flat, in his pocket. Shortly afterwards I flew back to Cape Town on my own, the Irish would follow shortly afterwards, I checked into the Camps Bay hotel, in a fantastic location 5 star hotel, the first day I walked a bit along the coast looking for a payphone, I found one and just when I want to make a call suddenly a black man passes me with a machine gun!! who then takes position behind a concrete bench a few meters away from me and with his barrel towards a row of shops, I thought, nice, a bit of excitement and sensation, maybe a hostage situation or something, then on the other side another colorful figure with a machine gun that takes place behind a kind of dune, WTF I thought, but then it became clear, a money truck stopped in front of a bank in front of those shops and there got yet another guy out with a suitcase tied with a chain to his wrist, he too was armed with a revolver, this one walked into the bank, and the black men were gone as quickly as they had come, in total there were 3 who apparently drove ahead with another vehicle.

Pooh I thought, South Africa is a bit different from the Netherlands, the days after that I noticed that weapons are very common in South Africa, but it was still weird to see a father playing with his child on the beach and dad wearing a holster including gun over his swimming trunks, but those are normal scenes in SA, as soon as I plunged into the soft drugs world in SA I would see dozens of guns, if not hundreds, everyone I met or was going to do business with carried a gun [or two] and often an arsenal in their homes too, and I didn't have a paring knife yet.

Feared me slightly, we were busy in bits and pieces trying to get around the one and a half million rock-hard old-fashioned Dutch florins there. I had already seen a land of great contrasts during my honeymoon, if you drive from Cape Town Airport towards the city, on the left you will see a gigantic township, a sea of corrugated iron roofs, and then once on the right side of the city, Camps Bay, Clifton, Somerset west, only villas one even more lush than the other. David came over with another Irish mate of his named Winnie, they arrived a few days later and we first sat down with Paul to discuss the possibilities, soon I realized that Paul clearly claimed a prominent position in the whole adventure, wanted to arrange a warehouse and the rental cars offered himself to guard our money even, too prominent for us, if you give an "outsider" that position you make yourself vulnerable, by that I mean you give such a person too much power, he can also pull the plug if he is not satisfied with his cut or wages for example, on top of that we were busy with an away match.

Shortly afterwards we travelled to contacts of Paul in Pietermaritzburg, a bloody long way somewhere around 1000 miles. Once there a friendly dude received us, nothing special really, they are all friendly when they can do business with you, also a motorcycle club related figure, he showed us some samples, expensive and dry brown messy material with seeds, and the buds were crisscrossed, not a success story in short, I also realized that he was a middle man who also got it from a middle man, annoying that the Irish also realized this and in unmistakable words babyface made this clear too me, so basically I looked like a dick, i mean we had previously flown 11,000 km and drove a car for 15 hours for this? This i also vented to Paul, his reply was that the lesser material was because it that this was trade from last season, and that the new harvest was ready within a few weeks, furthermore the man who brought it was indeed the owner of the trade he said, was bullshit, we had gathered that from the telephone conversations they had in the garden, well we had shown our teeth, he knew now that we were no amateurs. We drove back to Cape Town and decided to wait for the new harvest. I registered at a gym and because 'babyface' loved guns we went regularly to the shooting range to pass the time, and we drunk a lot of beer in Long street, Cape Town's nightlife area. When we received a signal that we could inspect new trade, we travelled to Pietermaritzburg again but before we made it clear to Paul that it had to be worth 30 hours of driving up and down, he was convinced that it was, we were not.

This time the trade was much better, but had to cost more than 400 guilders converted, a bit of a downer, in the end the first ton was ordered from the man, now it was important to rent a shed nearby and perhaps move there. Only as time progressed the cooperation with Paul became increasingly difficult, at first he was too frugal to shed a tear, except for a pistol never a Rand [local currency] in his pocket, Dave 'babyface' also wondered why Paul was so unbelievable tight by often saying in Paul's face " fuck sake Paul, I think a cash register fell on your bloody head or something when you were a kid", furthermore Paul sat everywhere with his ass in-between, could not one conversation take place without him being on top of it, in itself his right, they were his contacts, but along the way, eating bags of crisps and drinking soda on our expenses started to get annoying.

In the end, the ton we ordered turned out to be too "good" to be true, there were less than 600, which in

"The Camps Bay hotel Cape town"

itself was ok because we had not yet found a suitable warehouse, these postponements, or too little trade, I simply had to get used to that, because in the end I flew up and down at least 15 times and drove thousands up on thousands of kilometers through that South Africa. If you ordered a ton in NL around that time, you would have it on your doorstep in an hour, so to speak.

Finally, months later when we found a secure shed in Amanzimtoti along the coast road towards Durban, where we were latterly the only white tenants in the whole industrial estate, we bought about half of the trade from dude in Pietermaritzburg, then I started working on my camouflage by growing a beard and buying a flat cap because I had to order 1000 doors enough to fill a 40-foot container. And that camouflage, for what it helps, you shouldn't make it too easy for them.

Then there was a problem with Paul and his colleagues, upon inspection of the trade that was stored in the shed, we had discovered mold spots, which gives the weed a musty smell, there was at same time few hundred thousand outstanding bill towards man Pietermaritzburg, of course headache story, inspecting all the trade, opening it up, separating and exchanging of course, well Mr. Paul did not see anything in that, had a few strong words with the man and we returned trade for the amount that was open, and thank God that was quite similar.

We were done with Paul, and he with us, and I think in hindsight much better, because David and Paul didn't get along at all, and neither of them had easy characters. In the end it was a good decision not to let Paul arrange that shed and our rental cars, he did not even know where our shed was. Problem was we were only halfway, we had less than 2 and a half tons of trade ready, and in terms of contacts we were back to square one.

David and his soldier flew back and I started practicing how to arrange the other two and a half tons, well I had been in South Africa for months and remembered that in a mall I had met a very pretty dark lady in a souvenir shop in shopping mall the Waterfront, after I bought her souvenir shop empty to impress, I spent a day (and night) with her and she introduced me to some friends, a local gang, all "ganja" smokers, not that I had dropped anything that I actually did there, but maybe it was time to do some fishing in that group. Had dinner with her in the Cod father, a delicious fish restaurant near the camps bay hotel where I became a regular. I made the proposal, or so it felt, "*you are looking for ganja?*" She says, she was not stupid, and told me that she had already realized that I was not just a tourist, she could introduce me to a local who she thought could arrange something, told her that it was for more than a few grams, even more than a few kilos, all excited she says "*Tons*?" I "*could be* " the next day she introduced me to a dark lad who made a serious impression, he told me to go to Johannesburg to meet his mate. I say *to Johannesburg? That trade comes from the east side of the country, Swaziland, Durban, right? "No man, all over the place*" I think traveling again, Johannesburg, phew, maybe it's nothing, he saw me doubting, and says, "*listen, if there is somebody in South Africa who can arrange it, it's him"*

I agreed, I mean never shoot is always missing, he called the man on the spot, made an appointment for me and gave me a number of what turned out to be one of his employees.

One of the next days I caught a flight from Cape Town to Johannesburg, was picked up by a friendly dark dude and we drove together for an hour or so to a residential area called Observatory.

Arrived at a beautiful villa, a white dude opened the door and welcomes me friendly, *"Rodney is my name, but you can call me Rod,* there were children playing in the pool, his wife said hello while cooking in the kitchen, *"make yourself at home"* he says, offered me a beer, I doubted, I think this story is starting to take too long, *"no thanks"* *"to the point"*, I said;

"I've been driving through this country for six months, and I have investors breathing in my neck, i want to have this sorted, can or can you provide me a couple of tons off weed? And if you can show me some qualities, prices, and if yes could you bring it near our warehouse near Durban?" *"Everything is possible "* he asked the man who picked me up from the airport something in Afrikaans

Then he says *"Its maybe better you stay for dinner because i just told him to pick up a few samples"*

Once he was back, he gave me a plastic bag, it smelled good from a distance already, a sort of sweet smell, the smell of fresh weed, I looked in the bag, this was exactly what we were looking for! Not that dry messy brown full of seeds stuff, beautiful parallel decumbent softly pressed buds, light green, and brown where it had to be brown, the gear was completely shiny, stuck lightly, I was completely satisfied, although I did not show that to him *"looks like* it "I say, took off a few buds and saw that there were seeds here and there, showed this of course to him. *"How much"* I ask *"1200 Rand"*, that was around 320 guilders at that time, without that fat Paul this time, nice! And for 100 Rand per kilo, it could be brought to Durban near to our warehouse. I told him that our money had been there for months, hundreds of thousands of Guilders, Sterling, D-marks we had flown in, or via "hawala" -12%! The underground banking system I felt that we were going to finish the whole adventure with this man and had auxiliary troops come over from Amsterdam. His name was Stef, a loyal kid who likes to help, was not afraid, and like everybody wanted to earn some extra.

During dinner with him and his family, we went through some details about the logistics side, payments, etc., he said that the order, which in the meanwhile had shrunk from two and a half tons due to all costs, to 1800 kilos, could be arranged within 2 weeks. Turned out it was often time to wait again, I had arranged 2 hotel rooms in a hotel in Gauteng, which included a gym, casino, so we did not have to get bored.

Yet those 2 weeks deadline were not met, so I changed rooms in the hotel every now and then, different views, I also told the staff that I was military adviser, because after a few weeks they start asking questions anyway. Once the pile of merchandise was growing Stef started to sleep in the shed where he guarded the gear and besides that he also weighed and vacuumed the trade. By the way, he did that sleeping there with some mufflers supplied by our supplier, a shotgun and a revolver, not the latest stuff, but it bangs, gives a little more peace of mind instead of leaving 4,000 kilos unattended in a shed. Nevertheless, our man from Observatory also had to postpone sometimes, so Stef and I decided to go for a day to Soweto, the largest township in South Africa. Our supplier thought we were crazy. *"What do you want to do between those kaffers?"* He said, Kaffers is a swear word from white South Africans for their bronzed fellow citizens. Me and Stef thought, fuck it, looked at the map, it is gigantic, it is a city on itself with about one and a half million inhabitants. We drove in our rental car, and the more you drove into Soweto the more they twisted their necks, they looked at us as if we were aliens, in certain neighborhoods they warned each other by given signals, maybe they thought we were undercover police, under the influence of our own supply-high on our grass-we waved and kept smiling at everybody. We parked in the middle of Soweto on a square which was surrounded by restaurants and sat down on terrace and really I had not seen one white person except Stef since we were in Soweto, and the people were all so friendly, these people thought it was fantastic that we had come all the way from the Netherlands to see their Soweto, of course with the reputation Soweto had they had never seen a tourist in their life in Soweto, they were almost honored, in the end, the beer flowed freely, and we had an unforgettable

evening, the whole neighborhood was on our lips, we drove back completely pissed and got lost, the best thing was that we drove out with a Soweto police escort .. back to that boring hotel where I heard that our man had the last bits ready for us One of the last days I experienced a freaky thing at the hotel, after I entered my room from breakfast there was an owl in my room, between my bed and balcony, of which the doors were open, wasn't a small owl either, I estimated it to be about 40 to 50 centimeters, it looked straight at me, seemed almost like frozen the only thing I saw moving were his eyes blinking. I clapped my hands, and shouted at the bird, did not want to go, flapped at it with the blankets, the bird just did not leave, eventually I called one of the chambermaids in, she enters the room and sees the bird and the woman starts screaming, and ran out of the hallway I thought, probably a very dangerous kind of owl or something?

So I walk down to the lobby and tell a white manager about the owl and asked him why the chambermaid ran of like she saw a ghost, he had to laugh and said that indeed for the locals it is a bad sign, an owl that reveals itself especially during the day and on top of that inside, is so special that they say "sleg geluk" to it, bad omen, I say back home it is the other way around if you see something special such as a shooting star that you can make a wish.

The owl has been chased away by the maintenance, and I was wondering if this owl would bring happiness in this whole story, well the cover of the book already reveals how it ends, from now on I also scream and run out of the hall when I come across an owl in my house during the day.

The last trade was delivered, eventually 500 kilos less than planned due to all the delays and extra costs. For days afterwards with a jigsaw, removing the insides of the doors, leave the bottom 3 in one piece put some sawn out frames on top, trade in it, then close of with untouched doors, three of those pull straps over it, cover everything with plastic, ensure that all stacks look exactly the same, then call the logistics company to pick up the container.

Flew back to Schiphol, but what i I didn't know then, never to return. On arrival in Ireland, something was already wrong, the container arrived, once there were a number of "firms" waiting to divide the load but one of the boys noticed there was something wrong with the seal, it was different of colour, or different positioned, though they checked the whole area on the presence of police which they couldn't detect but most men left because they knew something had to be wrong, 'babyface' didn't want to believe it and send a few of his soldiers in and they had to pay dearly, there was an Irish observation team on it, then that front page article, "Biggest haul" needs little explanation to investors

THE IRISH TIMES

Gardaí have put on display the 4.6 tonnes of cannabis seized in Portarlington, Co Laois on Friday night. The cannabis is estimated to be worth around £9.2 million.

Four men were arrested and are being held under Section 2 of the Drug Trafficking Act. One of the men is from Dublin, one from Cork and the other two are from Tullamore.

The drugs were concealed within the doors of a metal lorry container which arrived into Dublin Port on Thursday. The consignment is believed to have originated in South Africa.

I still saw Dave babyface regularly, lived in one of the holiday houses next to the A2 near Vinkeveen just outside Amsterdam he had shifted his interest to "brown"/heroin, not my thing, and he wanted weapons, I introduced him to a Kurdish guy for both, lost contact with him, spoke another Irishman who said that Dave had an appointment in Ireland where he and his right-hand man both went, after that both of them disappeared, no one ever heard of either again, live by the sword, die by the sword story I guessed back then.

Years later I found this article in the Irish media

Independent.ie 🦢

David 'Babyface' Lindsay (36) and Christy Gilroy, both 36, are suspected of organising the murder of Anthony Foster, (inset) whose inquest has been adjourned. Foster (34) was shot dead in Coolock three years ago. Gardai requested the adjournment, informing Dublin City Coroner's Court that the investigation into his killing is live and is progressing.

However gardai are also certain that two of the central characters in his murder have been murdered too. Sources have revealed that convicted cannabis dealer

Foster was shot dead on the orders of major league drugs trafficker Lindsay. The Herald can now reveal the full details behind Foster's murder – a gangland hit which led to the gruesome murder and dismemberment of Lindsay just a week later.

In the summer of 2008, Baldoyle man Lindsay was at war with his former associate – a north Dublin crime kingpin nicknamed 'The Panda' – over a massive drugs debt that 'The Panda' owed to him. Sources say that Lindsay decided to teach 'The Panda' a lesson and ordered the murder of the gangster's close associate Anthony Foster, who was shot dead in the stairwell of a block of flats at Cromcastle Court in July 2008. But less than a week after Foster was murdered, 'The Panda' engineered a diabolical double-cross that led to the murder of 'Babyface' Lindsay and Lindsay's pal Alan Napper.

Sources believe the feared duo were murdered in a house in Co Down after being savagely tortured. After they were shot dead, it is understood that their bodies were cut up and dumped in the Irish Sea.

"Mister B. "

I wanted to buy my first property in 1990 and because of course, I had no income at all on paper, Rob B an tax specialist was introduced to me

B. had an office just outside the city and when I first got there I immediately saw that it was a coming and going of acquaintances from the world I came from who had the same problem as me, "too much" cash but too little on the bank account.

Once in his office, B told me that was no problem and indeed not much later he came by with a director of a local bank and after I gave a thick envelope of cash the property was appraised to which I then had to sign a pile of papers and I had my mortgage on a six floor building.

About ten years later I bought another four-floor building just around the corner from the first building in a similar way.

Peter shot to death in his car

This building was owned by Peter Petersen who I knew from the cafe de Halls

A savvy businessman that Peter, because I could not buy the property within a term drawn up in a provisional purchase contract, so he imposed a fine of 25,000 € on me.

Peter apparently did business with shady characters because not long after the purchase of the four floors he was shot dead in his BMW in front of a hotel that I cycled past for years as a little boy to go to school.

Thirteen years after I bought my first property, Rob B was arrested and after the man had been in custody for several months I was summoned to the police headquarters.

Once inside the station, I was overheard by two detectives who asked if i ever had worked for Rob B

"What kind of work, if i may ask? as a gardener?" knowing that Rob lived in a villa outside the city.

Mr. S don't kid us you got a mortgage through B. And signed a work contract as a consultant at a consultancy.

Well (ironically) that's weird a consultant at a consultancy, but no I say, I have given people advice, but not from behind a desk, usually at the bar or in a pub to people to call a taxi if they were drunk and not to go driving.

"So you never worked?

"no, never, and for sure not for B."

"Then why did you sign?"

"Say Mr. Police detective, that Mr. B came to see me",

[I look at paperwork]

"13 years ago now with a pile of papers and an appraiser, a long long time ago, and he says to sign here and there and you have your mortgage, so I sign, isn't it nice?"

"But you read before you sign, right?"

"Sure yes, listen, there were 40 sheets of paper, I put about 15 signatures, I'm not going to read everything, all those conditions, all those fine print"

"I find that unbelievable" says one of them.

[Me] "And you, you go and read all that when you go to the bank?" i asked rhetorically

"Yes, I do"

"Sure, you take all those papers and sit next to the coffee machine for an hour and read all that fine print?"

" you know what, that i find that again unbelievable" What are we actually talking about? "Thirteen years ago, I have had this mortgage closed with another bank for a long time, and it has also been paid for a long time" Man saw that there was little to achieve and ended the interview.

"Cowboy lawyer"

I met Evert Hingst via Rob B. for the first time in the summer of 2001 on the terrace on the back side of the Hilton hotel.

Strange bird with a smooth chat, neat suit, but just a bit different, sort of 70s style with trousers with wide flares with a perfect fold in them and expensive Italian sneakers underneath, it clicked with him immediately, I generally have a click with people who are different. After that I regularly visited his office called Toenbreker lawyers, but except for a case in which 105 kg of hash was found in one of my houses and for which I was fined 5000 € and 240 hours of community service which in itself was an achievement, but otherwise he never assisted me in any criminal case, for this case I paid him 5000 €, further he regularly sent me a text message to have a drink or a cup of coffee in the Utrecht street near his office, in his messages by the way he never used any spaces in between the words, like-comeandgrabadrinkwithmeatsameplaceaslasttime-   Shortly after a story where i went through the eye of the needle involving 14 tons of hash in Antwerp [*Plast&Nap*'s] where he by the way didn't know anything about he asked if I wanted to pass by his office, he wanted to show me something he said, he knew that I was good friends with Kees Houtman, and once in

147

his office he wore as usual another beautiful outfit, neat 3-piece suit along with cowboy boots with shiny points, the same kind of style buckle on his belt from silver and emerald and the lapels of his shirt also encrusted with silver and emerald as if he had walked straight from the Dallas series but without the hat. Also It seemed that the man had a different Rolex on his wrist for every day of the week,

"Come, walk upstairs with me" he said

Once upstairs he hands me a thick envelope, "here for you, or rather for your friend Kees, isn't he a good buddy of yours?" "Yes, I only don't see him much , he is under high voltage so to speak" I open the envelope, and its is full of tapped conversations from Kees and also from Ferdinand v d H, alias our Ferry, the director of our company, the company that had tried to get 14 tons of hash into Belgium for us, and "coincidentally" the tap conversation reports of Ferry were on top of the pile, i started to read the first pages, "do you know that Ferdinand too?" Hingst asks, "sure" and I told him the whole story about my narrow escape while he listened attentively leaning back in his chair with his cowboy boots on his desk, also Kees was discussed, how he was doing, in hindsight a very strange conversation, especially looking at the momentum, I had a large clothing store in the center of the city of which he knew was a pain in the ass, he offered to settle everything about this shop and to use the address of his law firm as a mailing address, I maybe have given him another two or three thousand for this

I don't know how much work he had put in to me, but surely a lot, why I wondered later, I was just a small client of him compared, for example, dudes with allure Mieremet who probably paid tens of thousands to him and especially when i heard from Rob B that the boss of the law firm , Toenbreker himself wasn't happy at all with Evert using the office as the mailing address for my bisniss, i wondered why I was in such a privileged position? Was it perhaps true what later in some media outlets appeared that he played a dual role as not only a lawyer but also informer of certain investigative organizations?

Could be because maybe the police thought I was a big kingpin who brought in containers full of drugs, big clothing store in the center which i bought from Sicilian "mafia" to perhaps "launder my money "and which i was busy selling to another group of Sicilian "mafia"

Truth was totally different, I've never brought in 1 gram of drugs with containers and the store was as good as bankrupt, and on top of that i was talking to Hingst like a headless chicken because I was pollinating my membrane every 10 days or so.

Not long after, Evert's office was raided and 500,000 euros and a gun were found in his safe, because of this incident and something else that had happened shortly before, namely he had top criminal Mierenmet come to his office and once mieremet left his office there was a hitman waiting outside, he was riddled with bullets but survived, later Mierenmet stated that he knew Evert had set this up, because he had him come to his office for something futile and once Mierenmet was outside, Evert quickly pulled the door into the lock according to him.

So I made a joke so now and than when I left his office by saying if I could look first through the half open door and sometimes i said ; "please don't close the door too quickly

March 11, 2006 , 19:47

The 36-year-old Hingst was shot at close range with a machine gun in front of his house in Amsterdam South at the end of October. The gunman had been waiting for the victim in a Jeep in the street for some time. The car was later found burnt out. Police say at least two people were in the jeep, but more may have been involved in the murder. The former lawyer is said to maintain ties with the underworld.

According to a spokesperson for the Public Prosecution Service, the investigation is still in full swing and the Public Prosecution Service wants to "keep control of all the evidence". Moreover, the judiciary is afraid that the images will be released when they are returned. "That is not in the interest of the investigation." The Public Prosecution Service does not want to say who the images behind me Evert" he didn't really appreciate these jokes by the way.

But after finding that money and the weapon in his office he was all over the national newspapers and I took a distance from him, I mean I have nothing against hanging out with someone who is "hot", but he was out of proportion that hot. Not long after on the 31st of October 2005 he was shot dead in front of his door while locking his scooter, I was reasonable shocked when I heard this , it was a special dude, there are never enough of them, Mierenmet gave an interview the next day by phone to a news outlet and said " that's where he belongs between the garbage bags"

And three days later on the second of November it were both Mierenmet and Kees their "turn", Kees in front of his door and Mierenmet in Pattaya Thailand, but most of these settlements of victims that I knew were when they returned home or in their immediate living environment.

"Evert shot to death between the garbage bags"

"Me my misses and a cup of tea"

In the early years of my marriage everything went smoothly, we just had a baby and we were happy, and in our large kitchen with an island, it was a coming and going of friends who came for coffee or a glass of wine, as well as weekend mornings when I spotted in the camera two men in front of my door, one was a long time acquaintance of mine from out of town, so I pressed the buzzer to let them in, in the kitchen the to us familiar H came in with a large oversized dude, he introduced himself as J., J gave me a firm handshake and after I took a quick look at him it was clear to me that J was working hard at the gym and accentuating his muscles with a bit of the old juice. "Coffee?" I asked...and while we were drinking coffee H explained to me that his buddy was experienced in making mdma powder, he asked me if I wanted to invest in an ecstasy adventure, and though I was easy to poke for a new project but in this case after some deliberation i thanked for it, when they left I took H aside in the hallway and told H who had a lot of experience in growing exquisite varieties of weed that I think it is more sensible that he sticks to what he is good at instead of

154

these wild adventures, words he would remember more than in one occasion he told me later, with melancholy he told me that for the moment they were going to set up a lab anyway with or without my dough, a few weeks later he stood at my door again in a very good mood, I let him in and he proudly throws a bag of powder on my table " we got it!!" He says, I looked in the bag and saw a slightly yellow crystal kinda powder, and since he knew that me and my wife were not averse to taking a pill every now and then, he asked if I wanted to try it out, I agreed and said that he had to wait a week or so for the result because we had to bring the children to their grand parents

When the time had come, my wife made a large pot of tea and i dissolved a small portion of the bag in it, we drank the tea very carefully and waited, 20 min, 40 min, nothing at all, then i put like half the bag in it, big gulp of tea this time, again waiting......nothing, we were done with it and resigned ourselves that there would be no "I love you so much" party.

A few days later H was at the door again and I handed him the rest of the bag and said "well done super lab technician"

He said he was sorry and that they had to adjust the formula, as soon as they were done he would bring in a new bag.

I agreed and again a few weeks later he was at the door with a bag of powder, only this time he had his arm completely bandaged and once inside he took off his hat and showed that he had no eyebrows and almost no hair on his head "WTF?" I say, "We had a little explosion in our lab" was his reply, "Little explosion? You burned half your freeping head and arm?" He waved it off like it was nothing, then the same ritual, children to grandparents, tea, powder in it, waiting , more powder, tea, wait ...... and again nothing.

Laughing I handed the bag back, and said "stick to your green fingers mate" (referring to his experience in growing weed)

Somewhat dejectedly he asked if we could try it one more time, "sure" I said, but of course I told him we couldn't keep on taking those chemicals to no avail.

Indeed a few weeks later he was at the door again with a bag and he assured me that this was the real mc coy, they knew where the error was in the process and they had adjusted the formula exactly as it should be "yeah sure you did" I said.This time the stuff has been in my house for a long time before we made a weekend off for it, not that crazy of course, we had given up hope a bit.

On a Saturday night in bed together the pot of tea came again and the bag in question, I thought I'd just dump the whole bag in it this time. My wife a cup of tea and I, we both zipped the cup of tea empty, this time the tea had a bitter taste, something we had not tasted before. Waiting again, 20 min, 30 min, we thought it's probably nothing again, and I poured us both another bowl, which we both drank, we watched TV, than i felt a slight change "Do you feel something?" I said, and while i looked at my spouse and saw she had pupils the size of saucers! from one moment to the next we were completely off the map., in the beginning it was still fun, holding each other, saying and feeling you are completely in love, really a typical ecstasy experience, but when it continued it became different, at one point my misses couldn't even talk anymore she just grinded with her teeth while her eyes were rolling in her eye sockets, she made noises just like a cat in heat that urgently needed and I didn't do much better, of course she had taken as much of that powder with her 60kg as I had with my 100kg, and it was starting to look like we had overdosed because when she wanted to go to the toilet to wee she couldn't stand, let alone walk, her legs were like elastic she flopped back on the bed every time she got up normally i could carry her to the toilet, but I couldn't handle that either at that moment, so i simply put a bucket next to the bed.

It should be clear that using ecstasy in this way is no fun.

I put gallons of water next to the bed and hoped that it will resolve by drinking as much water as possible to flush the stuff through our systems

Whatever happened but thank God it gradually got better, it only took days to feel like the old one again.

Not long after, H was at the door with J, I told them our story, they were completely ecstatic, finally they had the right formula, now they would market the MDMA in pill form, put their own logo on it and ready, they wanted to put in each pill 125mg, they told me they had 25 kg of powder which means they could make 200.000 pills, only problem was they didn't have a pill machine and if i didn't know anyone..."no idea" i said.

J said he might know someone who could flip the pills, and if they were ready if i could get them tested, because i knew a man called August de L, this was a man who tested the purity of the pills for a fee, and J promised me a drink for it. committed to acting as ginnipig and all the trouble, I agreed and waited.

Not long after that, H was at the door with a bag with about 15 light green pills, if I could have 5 of them tested, I agreed and a few days later I made an appointment with August de l., I handed over five pills and August said he would have the results within a week.

After 1 week I went by and paid and took the printout of the results with me.

On the way I opened the envelope and saw at the top it said 68mg on the first pill, the rest I can't remember exactly but they ranged from around 55mg to 115mg per pill so not one pill had the effective 125mg in it.

I put the results away at home and not much later J and H came by, "I have an unpleasant surprise" I said to them and put the results on the table, they both looked at it with wide eyes and J exploded " THOSE MOTHERFUCKERS, DIRTY DIRTY RATS!!!", he got so mad that I had to ask him to behave because my kids were both sitting in the living room watching TV, he cooled down, but it was clear that the man was totally pissed off., I quietly walked them to the front door and wished them luck and we agreed to see each other after my holiday in Thailand.

Shortly afterwards I went on holiday with some friends and had basically forgotten all about ecstasy, MDMA, pills and testing.

At one point we were all sitting at the pool in the hotel Clifton beach in Pattaya when one of my mates said. "Tjesus, you should read what happened back home" and hands me over the news paper, " the head was "Massive shooting in roadside restaurant" I read the article and at that time i had no idea that this had anything to do with the "party tea" i drunk with my misses.

I flew back to the Netherlands and late at night there is a knock at the door, I couldn't see in the camera who it was at the door so I asked via the intercom who it was " me H, open quickly!" I let him in and a totally upset man who lost a lot of weight begins to tell all over the show about his story,

"Have you read the papers??" he asks

"Yes, some, then what?"

"Also the one from the highway restaurant shooting?"

"Yes, I read that one in Thailand"

"Well, the one who got shot is J."

What?? Dead?!

"yes, riddled with 11 bullets"

H told me that after I had given the results of the pills J was completely gutted, he had these pills made by a father and son from Oss, an area where traditionally a lot of ecstasy and amphetamine is produced, J had the father and son both called to account after it turned out that there was far too little active ingredient in the pills, so J reasoned that what wasn't inside must have been stolen, he had initially invited them to a parking lot and wanted to have an explanation about the results that I had given them. It was denied by father and son and both assured that all the mdma powder had been mixed into the pills, driving J into a frenzy and screaming "EVERYTHING!?REALLY?! FUCKING 68 MG!!" apparently he and another free fighter body builder beats the shit out of the father from one side to the other side of the parking lot while yelling 68MG!!! J gave them a fine 250,000 and it had to be paid within a week of course.

The transfer of the fine would take place in the road side restaurant "de Lucht" where H acted as the driver of the two armed men, J and the other oversized gym boy, J had said to H (who was a bit scared compared to J) that he'd better wait on the other side of the highway for them to come back with the money.

What H did, H had no view of the restaurant nor the parking lot from there, he parked and waited, than suddenly a good 15 min later he heard police car sirens coming from all sides and knew right away that this had to do with his mate J ., he waited a little longer, but knew it was of little use and fled the scene, a few days when he was not present himself the police were at his door because his car had been filmed entering and leaving the parking lot just before the shootin The police wanted an explanation of his motives that day they told his girlfriend, he has been in hiding ever since and he asked for help selling the estimated 150,000 remaining ecstasy pills so we made an appointment to deal with the first 30,000 pills When he handed the pills to me he told me that he had already sold a few himself and customers had said they were incredibly strong and that I would do well to visit August de loor again, to which I agreed.

I brought 10 pills to August and waited for the results.

This time the results ranged from 2 pills even above 200 mg to somewhere around 65 mg again, I added the results of the 10 pills and divided it by 10,........and it came to somewhere around 120 mg per pill!

< **deVolkskrant** ∞

Four gunmen in De Lucht fired 37 bullets

The four men who opened fire on each other in the De Lucht roadside restaurant in Bruchem on Monday evening fired a total of 37 bullets.

From our reporter August 12, 1999 , 00:00

A 28-year-old man from Utrecht was killed in the shooting. His companion, a 24-year-old resident of Nieuwegein, is seriously injured in a hospital in Den Bosch.

Witnesses have stated that the two men who were shot at immediately reached for their weapons and that they also fired many shots themselves. The injured man is in stable condition, police said. Both residents of Oss were unharmed.

The two arrested men have not yet made any statements about the motive or motive for the shooting.

Nobody had robbed anyone, the stuff was "just" badly mixed, besides the father and son got convicted to in total 21 years, and the eleven bullets that J had digested which had cost him his life, and his mate who got hit by 7 bullets which he barely survived were all based on a miscalculating, nothing more nothing less than a misunderstanding.

"Another day at the office"

I bought a villa in Spain and there I worked with a firm, the leading figure was "fat P." who on his turn collaborated with an Irishman S.

They had a base in the Netherlands, a spacious apartment at the Loodrechtse Plassen 20 km from Amsterdam I considered them as friends, such good friends that we went on holidays to places like Zermatt a luxury ski resort in Switzerland, or to Solden in Austria and we stayed in the chic 5 star second best hotel in Austria, the Central hotel out there, we also visited champions league matches in Barcelona and Madrid, and to give an idea, we rented all 4 penthouses in the Arts Hotel close to the Barcelona port, and we had for some serious crazy money very crazy party's up there.

All in all it was an well-oiled organization that mainly consisted of travelers from the "garden of England", Kent, they had various transports from Spain, Portugal, the Netherlands and France, most off the time i couldn't find even enough merchandise for their needs, whether or Netherlands or in Spain, they always bought what was called soaps, a commercial type of hash, at least 3000 kilos otherwise the numbers didn't add up for them.

 At one point I was asked to come to Marbella by fat P, where he wanted to introduce me to a number of people, P. had many contacts, didn't work exclusively with me.

In a restaurant that was open 24/7 along the highway A7 that runs through Marbella, a restaurant that is known for its "cordero" leg of lamb from the oven, he introduced me to 2 neatly dressed Moroccans, and I don't mean dsquered jeans and a louis Vuitton bag.   They also spoke perfect English, something you hardly encountered with Moroccans in them days, without talking about birds and bees they came straight to the point, "we have send 14 tons of hash to Holland 4 days ago and truck and it's content and even the driver have disappeared from the face of the earth since the day before yesterday" , if I wanted to go to Holland to talk to someone who knew more about it and find out what exactly was going on, I agreed, and would fly to Holland the next day, they gave me a Dutch mobile number of the conscious person which I had to contact as soon as I was in Netherlands.

And just when i wanted to buy a ticket at a travel agency in Fuengirola a certain B. from Gibraltar calls me, this man was never discreet with the medium phone and just said over the open line that a friend of his had sent 8 tons to Netherlands and that the truck and the driver is missing, I think that's a coincidence, so I say "are those not well-dressed gentlemen from Marbella who speak good English?" He "no" and continues "do you want to go there and find out what's going on?" "Fine" "I said I have to go there anyway" so I ask him if he has a contact person and he gives me a number I think while I write the number down that the number looks familiar, the first 2 digits matched the number I had just had received from the 2 gentlemen, so I look to be sure, and damn! It's the same number! So I say, "this man of yours is not alone, or something is not right," "what, what you mean?" He says, Doesn't matter I say, "I'll fly there tomorrow". Once in the Netherlands, I contact "enforcer" N de J, a descendant from a notorious family in Amsterdam, a psychopath who stutters slightly, I tell him the story and ask him to accompany me to Brabant the province in the south of Holland where it all took place.

Made an appointment the next day with the great unknown who knows more about the missing 22 tons plus a truck and driver.

We met at one off the van der Valk restaurants in Gilze where a chubby friendly Moroccan with curls who after getting acquainted, quickly started to tell his story. He made the impression to be relieved hat he could tell his story, he also said that he appreciated our help The story was that the organization he was part of had rented a farm in Bavel in the name of a couple and that this couple was paid for every truck that got unloaded. Sometimes these trucks had to be picked up as the farm was quite remote, and in this case it was the first time the driver went to the location, so the male side of the couple had to guide the truck to the farm from the highway, this apparently had happened in the evening which was also confirmed by the dude himself who drove in front. But he lost the truck on the way, got lost in between two exits, drove a bit ahead according to his own words, but according to himself simply lost visual contact, the man drove back to the relevant exit where he had picked him up, but nothing, called the driver, like a hundred times, nothing. Completely disappeared from the face of the earth. I ask, how much was actually on that truck? Man quickly calculates...mmm...23 tons..

what? 23 tons!, I already noticed during conversation that he suspected the couple to know more about it, and at one point spoke it out loud, "the couple have tipped that truck away to people", the Moroccan continues, "guy had a prison past, and how can you lose a truck", he said, the driver was dead, no call nothing, not to his family nothing at all, maybe he was right about that I thought, he was also in contact with the owner of the transport company, he had not heard anything either, he told me truck color and model, Scania 480 hp, and added that this is a potent truck that can keep up well in traffic, so all the more, how can he lose it! He had also searched in a 30 km radius, nothing. In his eyes, there was only one suspect, that dude and his wife knew about it, there was no doubt about it. The man was visibly relieved, he got this off his shoulders, he had done everything he could and got a lot of telephone calls from owners, lots of pressure so to say, not strange we are talking about around 50 million euro wholesale value. The ball was in our court now, he said. First thing I suggested was to go and talk to the couple..... No, no, no, then they run away, we lose them forever!!. he said, something more rigorous had to happen, they had to be subjected to a forced interrogation or something like that he continued,   I took a break with J, *what do you think of the story?* Stuttering he said " *well i i i if you hear it t t the story they have to know more about it, he was the last person to see the driver and truck, and now driver and truck are missing, he is the key, so I say load them up.* Back at the table with Moroccan, *"ok, how? And where?*

 He said that they had not the slightest suspicion that they were the prime suspects, and that he was on good terms with them. Me: *"and how do they behave*?" Him: *As if their noses are bleeding, I even have keys to the house....J."oh can we take look over there?"* Moroccan: *when? J yes, now, tomorrow, as soon as possible, ...ok, wait, I call her,* and gesture to us to be quiet, me and J. listened as close as possible to the speaker phone , phone rings,..*Hey, hello, how are you*?   Says a seemingly friendly lady, *yes good*, says Moroccan,

 "are you at home this afternoon? I have to get something out of the shed", she: yes that's ok, we're away for a while, we'll be back at the end of the afternoon, she said a friendly goodbye and hung up,... a totally normal conversation, not even remotely anything strange noticeable about this lady, I   also said, for being part off a group nicking 23 tons of hashish and on top off that taking a driver hostage, a very cool lady, he: "hostage?! Man has been missing for 4 days, they have what they want, he is dead as a dodo!" Very likely i thought, where you need a witness for, even more so, i mean place yourself in her position, i said, to let a man disappear, means that woman must have nerves of steel, it was much too of a "light" conversation for such a serious case. Moroccan: well, they don't know anything, they just got tip money, they never really had a clue what was on such a truck for the Moroccan it was as Chrystal clear, it was them, "tunnel vision" they call it in police term ology, and we were all sucked into that tunnel of him.

 J. was also convinced, couple had to be loaded up, J. "do you have the keys?", Moroccan: yes in the car, J. Let's go and see before they possibly come back.

Once there, and indeed a back yard, also known as a dilapidated farmhouse, with a large wooden shed next to it that was locked with a padlock, first take a look in the shed, I noticed that the doors were actually small, I couldn't imagine that a 30 tons diesel truck was able to unload 23 tons of hash there, Moroccan also says, just fits with a truck, and sometimes not, and points to pieces of wood that are missing on both sides.

Inside I saw some lab equipment, I ask, what is that?, "oh that's a pill machine, and some other attributes to run pills" well I had never seen that before, unloading somewhere where there is also a kind of dismantled ecstasy factory, but in the south they apparently thought a little easier about it all.

Good so far, into the farm, J. looked around well as he pulls open the utility door and says, "h h h here it must happen mate", he walks up and continues, we hide ourselves here, as soon as they are in we mummify them in duck tape and load them into a van or something, and take them to a safe place nearby if possible. Yes, I say, where? " make some calls" he says , Well I say to Moroccan, we know enough, can you possibly lure them away so that we can hide? "Yes", he says, we were going to look for another location after all, so I'll come up with something. Great, then we'll drive back.
Moroccan almost panicked: but you will be here tomorrow, right?

Yes, with auxiliaries and a bill. Driving back I can remember that I did think about the telephone conversation between Moroccan and that lady, as relaxed as she was, still make me think, why if they have tipped that truck away why would this dude say that had seen truck and driver? Placing himself in the suspect's bench, I mean he could have said better that he had not seen him at all, so put the blame more on the driver, make it look like the driver run off but these were my thoughts, wouldn't match up anyway with Moroccan's and J's. Next day we met at the sloterplas in the west side off Amsterdam with J. There he was accompanied by his brother which I knew and another strange character, a little fat man with greasy hair and with thick jam jar glasses, I say "everybody ok?" , J. "Ah, just another day at the office", that jam jar said nothing, only nodded his head, while driving to the south he said nothing at all, except that he smoked one joint after another. I say "he is indeed quiet that buddy of yours, or is he just cracking on the joints?" Those brothers started to laugh, J. "but he's really good at what he does, and you know what's most important? " , "no, surprise me" i said J. "he doesn't talk!! " And man those brothers had a laugh.

We had another appointment at the same roadside restaurant, and afterwards we would meet G vd S, I knew him...me: S. Why?

He knows the ideal spot for the couple, about 50 to 60 kilometers from there.

First we saw Moroccan who was with an elderly man, man parked at same time as us and drove a Mercedes with

Luxembourg registration, this man was the owner of transport company and he expressed during our conversation that he was very concerned about the driver Whom at that time was already 5 days without a trace. I told the Moroccan of our plan, and what it would cost, and he agreed.

Then we drove to Belgium to meet S. who knew a farmer there with pigs during our conversation S. told us that we could rent one of his stables for 5000 a day, and that the farmer then looked the other way, and the pigs were included in those 5000.

We drive to that farmer, well that was not just any stable, more a complex of stables, farmer showed us around, there were stables for pigs with young, piglets, boars and I know what more. And it stunk, finally he took us to a stable that he had prepared, which housed adult bears, door open and he turned on the light, animals were apparently in the dark, what a stench, and as soon as the light came on those animals went crazy, the noise they made.. farmer: "I gave them nothing more to eat from last night after I heard you guys would visit me, and believe me they are hungry!

He took us further to the corner of the stable that was somewhat empty, he kicked the few remaining animals to the side and we looked at a concrete floor with a slit in the middle with a blade of hay here and there, finally he spoke the jam jar, he had noticed a handy detail in the floor, the floor had once been poured between wooden planks, and say the head of those planks were visible every about 50 centimeters, he said, " here chair, feet on planks", tap, tap tap, and made a movement as if he were driving a nail into the floor with a hammer. J. totally enthusiastic "Yes, yes good one!! Like that they can't they run away!!" Ha, ha ha, his brother was a bit more sober: "saves another pack of ty ribs". Farmer would no longer feed the pigs, "with skin and hair" he said. I paid S. the 5000 and then we drove back to Netherlands after first seeing our Moroccan.

Once I emphasized that tomorrow would be the day, and that he had to make an appointment with the couple around 3 o'clock, and had to keep them occupied for a few hours so that we had time to install ourselves there.

"All ok", he said, I got a deposit from him and we continued our journey to Amsterdam. Along the way, we discussed where to arrange van and talked over what the gentlemen had on their wish list of tools for the job.

Among other things, duck tape, ty ribs, banc lave hats, but J. still had those lying around, otherwise brother said he still had carnival masks, they also happened to be crook masks, "shall I also put on that striped jail suit also?? Ha, ha, ha, and what fun they had together.

Add a pair of pruning shears, Jam jar said, for the fingers and toes.

List was ready, van was arranged.

It did sink into me in the evening, this is a heavy story, but I pay so I decide, no fingers or toes are clipped, nails go between toes and

not threw feet, and we don't feed pigs and if they know anything they will say so, especially when they see a chair among a bunch of those hungry pigs. But also ran through my mind if they give up the names/connection of the people who are actually behind all this, where to go from there? if you have the balls to steal 23 tons of hash and make a driver disappear?, they could be really nasty people.

The next day we travelled with 2 vehicles, I was a bit tense, we had just started an unstoppable event, it didn't bother the brothers at all, they were as happy as 2 kids with a jar off cookies

Once there, the four of us went into a local hardware store, was really a clip from a movie, when I saw them at the cash register, pruning shears, ty ribs, I don't know how many rolls of duck tape, rolls of rope just to be sure, hammer and nails, the biggest out there, I thought when the girl behind the cash register really knew... The farmer also had given us a pig skewer, the kind of that gives a electric shocks.

Then again appointment with Moroccan who would ensure that they would stay away at least a few hour so that we could entrench ourselves at ease in the farm, he gave us keys and told us that we could go there with an hour. On the way to the farm, the brothers indicated that they first wanted to go to the supermarket to get beer and something to eat, it could become a long sit, so they said, i agreed.

Once there we left the car at the supermarket and continued with

the van and I also pointed out to jam jar not to turn the farm into a coffee shop, a bit strange when couple run into a cloud.

I drove a little further from the dike towards the farm so that no one saw them get out of that van, the three of them walked back out of my sight, I parked the van on the dike, the most strategic position I could find, I had a view of front of the farm, part of the driveway and the field, or meadow in front of it, but most importantly I had a good view of the road that led to the farm, I knew from the Moroccan which car the couple drove, a black BMW 3 series convertible, so now all we had to do is wait.

We had bought new disposable telephones and i was in contact with J. I called and asked if everything was alright "ah well "says J. brother " i got a space, it aint much, but ok comparing to jam jar is hiding in the meter box ", well as soon as you call I mean," we are now sitting on the couch with a beer and smoking a torch with jam jar". Me: "well then, the place must be completely blue of smoke, surely? " J. "don't worry, window is open". Me: "listen, when those people come in and smell trouble, literally, everything sucks" Clean up those cans and don't leave ashes or cigarettes behind."
"Yes, yes don't worry" J. said

1 Hour became 2, and I kept an eye on the road, and damn I see that BMW driving up!! I quickly call J. " hey mate in 2 minutes they are there!!
"YIPYYYYYYYYYYYYYYYYY!!" he yelled.

I brought binoculars and was about to use them, as it was a sunny day there were a lots of people with dogs walking around so I crawled back in the van so people wouldn't see me with those binoculars

The deal was that I would drive to the farm when the pair was muffed in duck tape, and J. would notify me when they were ready.

I look, and see the BMW parking on the driveway, and see both get out, she says something to him and she walks to the back of the farm, he opens the booth and apparently takes out some shopping bags and then walks to the back and i loose eyesight. After I don't see nothing for like ten seconds, suddenly i see that dud running across the driveway towards that field with brother of J. behind him!!! that dud was much younger than him and obviously running for his life, dude jumped over a fence like he was competing for the gold medal in the Olympics, brother off J. quickly gave up, i think WTF!!, I saw next to me a couple with dog watching the whole scene, i think fuck, better get out of here, J. call's me, "pick us up!

We got that bitch!!

Me: Leave her!! "We must have that dude, besides that way too noisy here! You run upstairs now!!"

I Picked them up, all three were completely gutted, brothers blamed the jam jar, which, as soon as he heard the door opening, jumped out of the utility box with his pig skewer ready to attack and had actually poked the woman with it, who had also screamed like a pig, the guy hadn't even come in yet and of course heard his wife scream and had dropped his groceries and made a run for it.

"she had shit in her pants too" the oldest brother said to the other, "yes, and he doesn't really love her either, the coward, leaving his bitch like that" J. said

Me "Yes, yes, all nonsense, half the dog club of bavel has seen us, and we have nothing, nada, zilch, because Moroccan would pay 45,000 as soon as we had the couple loaded up.

Called the Moroccan and told him that the "timing" was wrong and more technical bullshit, I thought I'm going to use professional terms to disguise our failure, and told that guy didn't get out of the car at all story, this whole conversation took place by phone somewhere from Utrecht, because I was finished with Bavel, Moroccan was sick, so were we, no dough, all for nothing, but many rolls of duck tape and pig skewer richer, I dropped the gentlemen off, and this was in the newspaper the next day:

De Telegraaf

Police intercept 32,000 kilos of hash

AMSTERDAM (ANP) - The police forces of Amsterdam, Kennemerland and Central and West Brabant have found 32,000 kilos of hash in recent weeks. Detectives intercepted consignments of soft drugs in various places in the country, which have a total street value of approximately 100 million euros.

Editorial11-04-06, 15:12Last update: 11-04-17, 06:33Source: destem

This was announced by the Amsterdam police on Tuesday. Agents rolled up a total of two international criminal networks that did business with each other. Eleven people between the ages of 28 and 52 were arrested. An investigation has shown that in the circles around the suspects at least three people have been killed as a result of violence. The violent crimes took place in the Netherlands.

The investigation started at the end of 2005 under the direction of the Amsterdam justice system. On March 28 of this year, the police in Zwanenburg arrested two Dutch men
aged 45 and 49. When a van and a warehouse were searched, detectives found the first 2000 kilos of hashish.

On April 1, the police intercepted a French truck, containing 7,000 kilograms of soft drugs and a loaded revolver. Officers arrested the two French drivers.

An investigation showed that the Frenchmen had already unloaded part of their cargo in Bavel in Brabant. There, detectives found 23,000 kilograms of hashish in a house and the associated storage facility. In addition, they found parts of an amphetamine laboratory and various raw materials for the hard drug. There were no people in either building at the time.

Later, the police in Best arrested a 28-year-old Spanish woman and a 40-year-old Dutch man. Two 32-year-old Moroccans were arrested in Oosterhout. In Brecht, Belgium, agents arrested a 32-year-old Frenchman, a 52-year-old Spaniard and a 39-year-old Moroccan.

So nobody had stolen anything, now it gets scary, I knew that every step we had taken had been photographed and or filmed, overheard.

By deliberately waiting to leak/inform the press, they created an ideal situation to arrest everyone who walked through this investigation. The couple from the farm, the Moroccan, the transporter everyone except us .. why? First of all, my guess is, we were not part of the organization that imported hashish with 23 tons at a time, secondly I think that if we had already been arrested, the mode operands of justice would have been wiped off the table by a smart lawyer, and maybe a very small chance and everything would be exposed in the open by the media.

Also 2 good acquaintances of mine were caught in connection with this case, big John de J and yet again Thomas v.d Bijl, where the old bill found 2 tons of hashish in his carpentry business in Zwanenburg, Big John spent 2 years in jail and Thomas was back on the street in 2 weeks, everyone knew then that he had a "separate status". Not long after that he was shot dead next to his vacuum cleaner in his/our pub De Hallen

"Judas Dog and the Revenge of a Pen"

The following story is about a 1.8 million euro theft and is dated August 21, 2007 and shows that what I also often tell my children that the real Judases are usually not the typical dodgy looking hooded figures on the street corner, but often come from the corner of acquaintances, "friends" or even family and show once again that there are real wolves in sheep's clothing who pretend to be your friend and nest around you, say, make a project out of you, playing theatre and in the meantime wanting to look as deep as possible into your kitchen, and all for one purpose; rob you

I was working with a Moroccan, a real operator at the time, the man was responsible for a lot and I mean a lot kilos (more than a couple of tons) of annual import of hashish to Europe. This happened in various ways.

Most of it was sailed with fast ribs over the Mediterranean Sea, some with sailboats and also yet skies and a lesser part was hidden between regular cargo such as containers from Casablanca and in this case the containers arrived in the port of Valencia.

The trade was very cleverly hidden, it was in very large spools of nylon thread, and I mean spools of 2.5 to 3 meters long, on both sides there were say 80 cm stainless steel discs, in between there were 60 cm thick nylon thread rolled around the shaft, at least for the eye yes, in fact there was a layer of about 10 cm on it because around the axis there were hundreds kilos of hash from disk to disk wrapped around the axis than again a layer of lead stuck over the hash so that nothing could be seen on the scanner, around each axis of each coil, depending on size of the hash was between 750 and 800 kg. Each time 6 spools were sent from Morocco and I had to receive them in Spain, remove their disguise and put them on further transport to the Netherlands. It ran great every few weeks I was up to my neck in hash, lead and nylon thread, only the empty spools went back to the factory in Casablanca for reuse.

At one point I get a call from an old buddy from Amsterdam, big J, he told me that someone urgently wanted to talk to me, a Gerrie or Gerrit. v.d S, I knew this one from cafe de Hallen, a nice guy at the time, laughed a lot with him. He would be waiting for me that evening at cafe maracas in the port of Benalmadena.

That evening I went to cafe maracas to hear what the vd S had to say.

Once there he greeted me kindly and offered me a drink, after a friendly short chat he got to the point.

"we have a problem that needs to be solved, and you can contact the people involved"

With his pointed face and his big nose (his nickname was the beak) he told me that he had invested in a company in Casablanca that sent trade to what turned out to be the same way as my Moroccan did, he called the company and the director his name and knew from a reliable source that we were now working with "his" company, so he accused us in fact, that the company, his creation, so he said, was working behind his back with us

He said that was unacceptable and wanted it resolved, with the threat of "if I don't make money nobody does" in other words he would tip the line away, snitch on the operation, and so be it, he knew more than enough about the company to do that. I asked him again how he came to know that I knew more about this, but he avoided answering by saying, "It doesn't matter, does it? You know the system in connection with the company and director, right?"

What I agreed, that was my first mistake, now he had a foot between the door.

"So how are we going to fix that?" he said

I told that I had nothing to do with the sending side, that I only handled Spain and the Netherlands, but that I was willing to contact the boss and inform him about the situation.

I called once i was back home to B aka "the butcher" in Morocco and told him the exact story, at first it seemed unlikely to him and he wanted to know exactly how I knew him and what else I knew about him.

Further he made no commitments and would contact company director the next day.

Early the next day the Butcher called me and said annoyed that it was a total bull shit story, the director had never heard of G.vd S, and offered to vd S to come to Morocco to and talk with the Director face to face

Since vd S was still in Spain, I met him again at the same location and told him exactly what the butcher had said, director did not know him, never heard of him.

"Of course he denies! You understand that, don't you?" was his response

In a way he was right, i mean when the director is eating from two plates he wont admit that so I suggested we go and talk to the director in Casablanca.

"listen the director speaks no Dutch, only Arabic and French, and he was just a pawn, i have never spoken to him, seen him maybe once or twice, , he knew the company is set up with somebody else's money" " and it is impossible for me to go to Morocco at moment" and made it clear he wanted a solution because he had to go back to the Netherlands.

I was not in a position to offer a solution I said and than he bet high by going all in.

"ok, fine, then we all make nothing anymore, not a penny"

I reassured him to keep calm and that I would contact the butcher again.

"Can you reach him now?" he asked

"Yes, I have a one to one phone with me"

"better call him now, I'm going back to Netherlands tomorrow, I want an answer otherwise the whole story will be going down this week"

I went out to call the butcher privately and was the messenger again

Butcher was not amused and we went through some scenarios together, of course it was clear to us that vd S was resentful, and he also knew the company name, he even knew the freighter who transported the container.

And we both suspected vd S of playing some kind of game but for the moment we couldn't get a finger behind his involvement, but the fact remained that he knew all the ins and outs of the business and therefore was in a position to do a lot of damage, so after some deliberation butcher offered that he could invest 500 kilos at Moroccan price on the next load, that was butcher's ultimate offer otherwise he had to do what he could not resist. Once inside I told of the offer which he listened attentively but with a difficult look.

After some mumbling complaints he agreed, he wanted to know when the next transport was and what he had to pay for the trade in Morocco, and how to pay.

I didn't know all that and because we had our communication run through third parties, we exchanged numbers and I promised him to provide the information as soon as possible.

We said goodbye and he seemed relieved, old-fashioned cheerful, as he used to be.

Very shortly afterwards he contacted me and i gave him the prices of different qualities in Morocco, the price for transport to Casablanca and for transport to Spain, I don't remember exactly but it came up for a middle class hash in somewhere 11a 1200 euros including transport , this material was easy to sell for 2000 in Spain and around 3000 in the Netherlands, a smooth 400 k profit in Spain, say 700,000 in NL because of the additional transport costs to NL.

He agreed, and after this deal was settled in hindsight Vd S was very communicative with me, every day he sent me messages how I was doing or what I was going to do.

Shortly afterwards he sent me a message that he would come over with his girlfriend for a few weeks and stay at Oceano Hotel just past La cala mijas.

It was early summer 2007 and vd S had arrived, my wife also stayed with me on the costa del sol, vd S was at my door from day one he arrived, yes, a bit strange, but i heard he had been struggling financially in recent years, so thought the guy was really happy with the deal in where I had played a substantial roll.

He was very communicative, calling every day, and whenever he could see, always friendly and full of jokes, almost every night he invited us for dinner in one of the better restaurants along the coast.

I didn't smell any harm, really nothing, something I did immediately when it was too late.

Perhaps the hairs on the back of my neck should have stood up when he asked questions about his participation in the project such as, "Do you guys actually have a strong arm when something goes wrong?" or again on another occasion "or "where in the Netherlands should I pick up his trade?"

But he did that very cunningly, maybe one question a night, and always with a bottle (or two) of wine.

But because he was, say, a partner in the "spool adventure" I didn't smell any danger, but in hindsight he of course wanted to get to know the organization, the strong but especially the weak sides.

I also went out with him into the "nightlife" of Torremolinos, among other things, there I can remember some different questions, whether I had never played a trick with my contacts, so whether I had always been honest, thought that was a strange question despite that we were both fairly drunk but had to disappoint him, no.

Also one evening he surprised me with a few grams of coke, he snorted and strongly insisted that I joined, I told that the fun was gone from me and I would run directly to the nearest brothel.

We also talked a lot about how I knew the butcher, and actually all kinds of information about him.

After a week he left and my wife pointed out to me that vd S was very precise because she often saw him take notes, something I had never noticed, so he apparently did that when I went to the toilet, but it didn't ring a bell yet. Shortly afterwards he and his wife left and I continued with my daily worries.

At a certain time I heard from the butcher that the spools would be sent again and he asked when vd S would pay, it was about an amount of around 250,000 euros, and then on top of that the transport had to be paid on arrival, he said, I couldn't do more than to contact vd S about this.

Vd S was delighted but could not give me an indication when he would pay the money but it would be fine and informed me that he planned to come to Spain anyway in the coming days and to inform me there.

I don't know where he found a hotel this time, but at least he slept with us the first night and there the Judas enjoyed the care of my wife through, among other things, an extensive breakfast.

The following days the same ritual, a lot of telephone contact, a lot of food and a lot of wine, about the 250,000 euros that he had to pay in advance to participate in the spool story was less clear, it was on the way, everything would be fine, he said.

One night out in a restaurant he started asking questions that should have ringed the biggest alarm bells, as it was now clear that he didn't want his stuff to be sold in Spain but transported directly to the Netherlands together with the merchandise of the butcher. he started with an story and said that perhaps it would be better that once the merchandise got delivered in the Netherlands it was better to unload in his warehouse, he had a super-secured warehouse so he said, and he also always had armed security guards on the lookout.

I immediately told that the butcher would never do this, he himself had three different locations throughout the country to unload, I said.

"yes, but are they properly secured? those locations, I mean it's also my stuff that gets unloaded"

You probably can already feel where this is going, the Judas was hearing me out in a very cunning way, little by little, because he never really asked pushy, he threw his rod every now and then, but he was still slightly more determent compared to his first stay.

I was of course under the impression that he was not aware of our locations so told him not to worry, but he really wanted to know why he shouldn't worry, and then I satisfied his curiosity and told him we don't have an electronic alarms at any of the locations, no noisy stuff one was permanently occupied, other location was for unloading and direct transit, so nothing was left behind and the third was mechanically very well protected, the fire escape which was a weak point but behind it was a forklift parked , I told him, now that I write it down my neck hairs are standing up.

He did not know which of the warehouses had what kind of security, but he now had a wealth of information which he could work out, the location that he knew beforehand and which he robbed was in an industrial area in Amsterdam-Sloterdijk.

Now he could puzzle with the info he had, of the three locations there was one where someone lived permanently I had told him, that could never be this one he wanted to rob, nobody lives there, and then the shed that was only used for unloading and transit which was located in the province, with the info he was aware of beforehand he knew that the shed in Amsterdam was also intended for storage, so it was now clear to him that the shed he knew the exact location of was not equipped with an electronic alarm and a very important detail that a forklift truck had been placed against the fire door on the back side.

Since we hadn't used that shed for 3 months, he had to know one more thing; the momentum.

That's where he completely focused on from that moment, he was on top of my case, all day messages and terraces, had his wife come over and would stay for a few weeks, he said.

He was extremely loyal at that time, went the most expensive fish restaurants, dining and wining every night on his expenses, i just couldn't pay though i offered going halves. every now and then a question about the security of the locations, the bastard Judas probably wanted to put a few more exclamation marks on his scraps.

Then it happened, I was called by the butcher to do a job in the Alicante area, 8 tons of hash would arrive there and that had to be put on transport to the Netherlands, and I would travel there in a few days, in the evening I saw vd S again in a Thai restaurant where he invited us, i told him i would be away for a few days to "do odd jobs"

"oh, ok should I help you there?" he asked directly, I thought it was a nice offer, but declined the offer, people there would not appreciate that a stranger suddenly walks around at their location was my reply.

He was very interested and I saw no harm in telling what it was about, 8 tons for the Netherlands, "ok, and when are you leaving for Alicante?" I would leave 2 days later, that was a Thursday and I told him that, "oh ok, well then I'll keep my fingers crossed for you" I'll stay here for at least another week with my wife" he said. (Afterwards I found out that he also boarded a plane to the Netherlands on that same day I left namely a Thursday)

Now it was counting for him and make a little gamble

192

This was the moment where the bastard Judas was waiting for, The goal he had in mind from day one, all he knew was a release location, everything else around it was theatre, all of it.

So on Thursday I travelled to Alicante, which is about a five hour journey, so he could almost certainly count on his fingers that Friday the eight tons would be unloaded in Alicante, if these were put on transport to the Netherlands immediately on Friday, the trade would arrive in Amsterdam Monday, more likely Tuesday, all he had to do was put a man in front of the door Monday and Tuesday, and to not miss out on anything on a Sunday to, and as soon this person sees a truck or van driving inside he knew the merchandise was there.

I did what i had to do and somewhere in a warehouse in the Alicante area me and two others received a number of transporter vans on Thursday afternoon, three to be exact, 7800 kilos were spread over the three, with the help of two others we divided the trade on pallets that were used as a deck load of rubber mats on that same Thursday until late in the evening, removing a number of boxes from the pallets to make room for the hash, the hash was divided over 28 pallets, in other words a complete truck. Then very late and completely exhausted I took a hotel nearby, the truck would be there around noon the next day.

Once in the hotel I called the butcher about the situation, then it came up to perhaps spread the risk to bring the load to the Netherlands in two parts, I thought it was a better idea to have it delivered in two, less risk and the transport price remained the same, butcher didn't really care, but after some insistence he agreed, which meant that I had to be present in the shed a little earlier to adjust the freight.

No sooner said than done the next day, and after we were sure that all pallets looked exactly the same, we received the truck that would bring the load to the Netherlands.

This driver, incidentally, was aware of what he was driving.

Late that same evening I boarded a plane from Valencia airport to the Netherlands. This late flying on Friday was more convenient because I wanted to be on time for my son's birthday, which would take place that Sunday. (That's why I still know exactly what day it was after all these years)

During the birthday I heard that the truck would not arrive on Monday but Tuesday, also somewhere around noon. Together with a certain P (who most likely unwittingly played a role in this theft), I finally unloaded the truck in the warehouse in the province, and brought it to the warehouse in Amsterdam over two journeys during the Tuesday afternoon together with P.

This shed was a large shed, with an overhead door, around 100 meters deep and 20 meters wide and with a ceiling of around 8 meters high, on both sides were racks with pallets with a cubic meter of tubs that could hold 1000 liters of liquid material, at least 40 of them were piled up along the wall, these were empty, had once been used for the same tricks, furthermore there was a door on one side to a small storage room, toilet group and an office. It's important to get a sense of all this in connection with my "forensic" investigation later on.

We had often stored the trade in that smaller warehouse, to which we camouflaged the door with a two-meter high stack of pallets.

So we did the same with the 3.6 tons of hash.

At the end of the day we were ready and we closed and agreed that we would both be present at 10 o'clock tomorrow morning, P had the keys and the shed was also registered in his name.

After dinner I lay down on the couch and I get a call, I look at the screen...vd S, I answer "hey mate how are you? Are you going to do something fun tonight?" Surprised I ask if he was back in Amsterdam yet, he admitted and told he had just landed that afternoon because his wife had to come back for a relative. I told them I was wrecked and going to bed early.

"Okay, in that case I'll also stay home "

The next morning I was just about to get in my car to drive to the shed I get a call from P, I pick up...totally upset he says " WE ARE RIPED!!" I say dumbfounded "what, what do you mean?" He then told me that the overhead door was open when he arrived, and that the normal door next to it on the left had been broken open with a crowbar, there was still the crowbar and a shovel in the shed, I said I would come as soon as possible.

Once I have arrived I see P on the other side of the street with a say, worried / startled look.

I also saw as he said that the doors were like he told me

We walked together to the shed, and I ask "is everything gone?" He replied that he hadn't been in yet, and made a gesture of that i had to go and have a look.

I think he was so depressed and or afraid so I went to look first, it was a mess all the plastic 1000 litre pallets had been pulled from the racks, piles of pallets pulled over, and also the pile that camouflaged the door to the office and the small storage, all the lights were on, and the 3.6 tons had been stolen, there was not a gram left, the drawers in the office where also about 10 kilos of examples were emptied, everything of value was taken. P had already joined me, and said "how the fuck, and who the fuck, we didn't use this location for almost three months!!"

I don't know if I answered or if I said anything at all.

I walked with him through the shed trying to make chocolate from what I saw, everything had been knocked over so the thieves didn't realize they had to be in smaller storage in the office, furthermore truck tire tracks could be seen, a large double axle truck was used to load the 3.6 tons, which on itself is strange, 3.6 tons you could also load with a big van, i know, did it myself many times, and more even, so why a big truck?

The same truck also stood a meter parallel to the shed front, this could be concluded from the tire tracks, the back door where the forklift was standing was untouched, at least from the inside, I was curious what could be seen at the back, if you If you want to break into this location, that fire door is the most logical, in contrary to the front the door is located in

196

a narrow alley, no car traffic, and there is no view of it, from anywhere.

Once at the door i noticed it was completely untouched, not a mark on it, stronger than that on both sides there was some vegetation to say hip height and there were even spider webs hanging in between, so this door had not even been looked at. I thought that was really strange. Despite communicating with v d S during all that time not a single alarm light came on, so filthy smooth and refined he had played it, but soon that would change, one after another alarm bell went on big time, I went into town to buy a new sim card and phone to call the butcher, I have to admit that I was badly shaken, the moment I drive into town v d S calls me and asks how it's going, I told them that I was in deep misery and that we were ripped. "NO REALLY?! Can I do something for you? Where are you? I told them where I was and in no time he was there," what the hell! How is that possible? I shrugged and I don't remember what I said, then he said, "ill help you with tracing the material, surely the material is getting offered somewhere, what were the things that were stolen, was there a stamp on it? What's it worth? I told him what he wanted to hear, and because i was of the chart, i didn't feel like talking anymore, we said goodbye, he got into his car but didn't drive away immediately, he started to call in his car, but with two phones at the same time, he still had his window half open looked at me and closed his window and continued to call in his parked car in a very surreptitious manner, suddenly i knew, the coin dropped, he had done it, got in my car and played the whole Spain movieset to myself, WHAT A MOTHERFUCKING CUNT i yelled, maybe if he had never called me the previous night, and this morning, kept quiet, i would probably have suspected him at a certain moment, but those two phone calls, the one the night previous asking if i go out, and the one this morning and that strange suspicious secret phone call just after our meeting had betrayed him, as good as he had played it the first 4 or 5 months, but within 24 hours of the theft he had fallen through the cracks and the fact that he had played this so sophisticated I know this was his modus operandi , this wasn't his first job, impossible, this dude has done this kind of tricks many times already, That I was sure he was behind it I did not vent to the Judas /motherf*#%ng c☆▯nt, at least not that day and my suspicion would also be confirmed at a later stage from various sides about this Judas.

But from then on he called me every day and worse, he was regularly at my door to "express his condolences" but of course more to find out if there was any trace of the stolen hash and if we already suspected who was behind the theft, and I had to hear that shit from him while grinding my teeth.

 But I had agreed with the butcher to play stupid for the time being

 Of course I had contact with the butcher about the theft, of course I told him all my findings and also that I was sure that vd S knew more about it and I noticed after the first calls were more about disbelief and disappointment they changed the next day to more business-like, first of all the location had to be cancelled, it was infected, and although he didn't suspect me, there was slowly more pressure that "it had to be solved"

Word quickly spread about the theft as we were trying to locate the products, so at one point when I walked into the office of a large hash broker named P to ask if there was any news of the theft, he told me he had heard that there were also suspicions towards me, and that they came from the corner around the butcher, I was very nuanced expressed not amused when I heard that.

So as soon as I was outside I called him immediately and at least had a good argument "Listen Habibie (we always called each other Habibie which means mate) I've been working with you for years, never missed one gram, otherwise I hope you can remember our phone conversation when I stayed in Alicante to load your gear, it was you who wanted to send the 7.8 tons in one go, I was the one who said do it in half, think about that!"

After a few days there were indications that a certain part of the stolen trade was circulating in the southern provinces, but after some more research these roads came to a dead end, in the meantime Judas rung my door bell, told me "he was busy all day for me to locate the thieves" I had meanwhile bought a gun through all the consternation which was on the dining table, and the moment he entered he saw this immediately and while he sat down on the couch, he kept an eye on the gun while he puts one hand under his coat (i presume he was armed) and asked why I had a gun? "Listen mate, whoever pulled this trick on me put me in serious danger, I was the one stashed the trade there at night and in the morning it was gone!" Sure bit of a bluff, then his standard question came, "do you know what? Don't you have any info in a certain direction so I can help you?" Then I couldn't take it anymore, "yeah, we have" he jumps up in the couch while keeping a close eye on my gun and says, "what tell me? who?"

"I spoke at length with the butcher and he said that I should think carefully about who has been hanging around me for the last few months because he said this is the key person to this theft" for a moment he looked with his rat head very surprised, and says, "oh, can you think of anyone?" "Yes, you" I say, then completely bewildered he stood up and says "how can you say that!" and screaming "I am your friend, are you going to suspect me now?" "Yeah, it is what it is, you've been around me all this time, nobody else," then he walked away and slammed my front door with a loud bang.

Finally, he knew we knew, and it was against the deal with the butcher, but it saved me a lot of teeth grinding.

Of course, he never called or visited me again after that, but I did catch that he was trying to get the contact details of the butcher, rate face Judas was clearly concocting something else.

Since I knew/felt that he was working on something, I walked continuously armed and even moved to a place outside the city.

Meanwhile, the butcher told me he had hired a strong arm R a "notorious" dude from the city, i didnt know him personally but heard of him, everybody knew that this R once owned a brothel named Esther in Haarlem where Martin vd P aka Polletje was the doorman, and in the year 2000 shot and killed 4 men in that same brothel (R was not present at that moment) Polletje got arrested and after the prosecutor demanded life in imprisonment the Judge convicted him to 15 years because he believed he acted partly out of self-defence, a few years after his release he got killed himself when he brought his daughter to school.

R had also been in jail himself in a distant past because a Moroccan had "fallen" from his car at 160 km per hour which obviously he did not survive.

The butcher wanted me to talk to him and tell him all the details, which I did shortly afterwards, behind a car wash on the edge of town where he was waiting for me with a whole line of sordid types.

After getting acquainted, he immediately said that all options were open to him, everyone was a suspect, including me and P who had unloaded with me that evening.

I said that I thought that was strange because it was crystal clear that vd S was behind it and told the whole story in a bird's-eye view. "Do you have proof of this?" I looked at him funny and said "Why? Are you going on the detective tour?" And told that I at least still had the messages from the last two weeks before it happened which declared a lot

He gave me a hard look and says "If that's nothing it's your word against his word"

In the meantime, his accomplices tried to look as angry as possible, accomplices who, incidentally, were from the former Eastern Bloc, which I could tell from the few words they exchanged among each other

R ended the conversation and said he knew where to find vd S and would talk to him to hear his side of the story. I didn't feel a real relief from the conversation, and knew that a conversation with that rat vd S would do nothing, S would do everything to prove his innocence, and was nasty enough to put the blame on me or if necessary with his mum, so to speak.

In the meantime, my wife mentioned that she had seen vd S drive by our house a number of times and that the neighbor had warned her that she had seen two adult masked guys through our backyard the night before who had fiddled with the barn door.

Since the barn door was open, she checked the next day about something missing but she said everything was okay at first glance.

I knew these weren't just two grown dudes trying to steal a bike and my gut said this was related to vd S so I travelled straight home to examine the shed more closely, there were boxes piled up against the wall and after I moved maybe two or three boxes I found it, half a kilo of hash and after a bit of examination and a call to the butcher it was clear that it was from the 3.6 tons of hash that was stolen, the filthy rat was pulling out all the stops to put the blame on me that was clear.

And of course the expected call from vd S came shortly after, a call from vd S to R that he had indications that I was selling the stolen trade and that he had heard from reliable sources that some of the trade was stored in my shed and that R should not ask me about this but should call me and immediately order me to look in my shed.

I made another appointment with R who meanwhile said with a smile that he knew that vd S was behind it.

Finally I got some imaginary air, and knew that suspicion shifted completely to vd S where it belonged, but also knew from experience that when you "invite strong arms to solve a story it often gets a tail" and that is exactly what happened.

Then something happened that almost made me fall off my chair, the butcher called me and told me that vd S had managed to contact him via via and he told that he was in morocco and needed to speak to him urgently, butcher agreed and said that he was in Casablanca and even though vd S was in Tangier, that didn't stop him.

The Judas had thereby shown that he was not only in a corner, but also that he was not afraid.

The location of the appointment was because it was an away game for vd S therefore determined by vd S and this was in the MC Donald's Ain Diab on the paseo maritimo in Casablanca, not really a suitable location to kidnap someone or otherwise.

There vd S appeared with not one but two men and as expected he denied everything and tried to put the blame completely on me, he really pulled out all the stops, I was a sniffer, a junkie, involved in more of these similar thefts , and above all he would soon come with indisputable proof that I was behind the theft, the butcher told me after the appointment.

Now I understood why he asked me at the very beginning when we were drunk (or at least me) if I had always been clean on the degree, never played any tricks, had I had any tricks at all and i would have shared them with him he would be able to hit me with that now, everything, really everything he'd asked for in the past had a reason.

Knowing the butcher he must have listened quietly and certainly did not show the back of his tongue, yet I asked what he had said to him. "Nothing Habibie, I only listened" strangely enough he asked me right after, "hey Habibie, listen, you didn't do this together with this dickhead did you?"

I told him he was out of his mind, why the half of 7.8 tons and half of that again if I could have taken everything.

When that Judas dog was back in Holland, what I heard he walked around armed and armored, from someone close to him I heard that he was wearing two glocks in his shoulder holsters, a bulletproof vest, he even had a kind of shoulder bag with a long flap on the front side. which was also bulletproof, even a sort of bulletproof cap if I had to believe it.

It was clear that he himself realized that his bluffing stupid bullshit hadn't worked.

Shortly afterwards R also travelled to morocco to meet the butcher, once together the butcher turned out to have said on a whim that the vd S had to die, nothing strange about something like that after what the vd S had done, this statement would only be of great implications for the butcher as these were apparently recorded by R or one of the men he had with him that day.

As it turned out, the Judas had established good ties with R, he had proven to be good at manipulation, but he also had money, after all, he had just stolen a little under two million, so I personally think he got R into his camp that way, the recording of the butcher wishing the death of the Judas came to the ears of the Judas himself (could be very likely that in the recording there was a lot more to hear then just wishing him dead) and both made the diabolical plan to extort the butcher and forced him to pay half a million, in the end this became three hundred thousand, this whole story came to my ears much later, butcher has told me this himself, I almost fell off my chair when I heard this, I was dumbfounded, after some time I said to him "now you dug your own grave in business, in the city they know that you have been robbed by the same one that extorted and you paid!! Now you're running game!"

My prediction was not far off, because shortly afterwards, when the butcher wanted nothing to do with me business wise, he was robbed twice, E a person who was closely related to Judas (which the butcher didn't knew) offered him a transport from Spain to the Netherlands, the deal beautifully disguised, fetched him at his house, tempered him, build up trust, to which butcher finally agreed. The trade was issued in Spain, but never arrived in the Netherlands. BENGGGGG, the butcher lost almost another four million. As if that were not enough, the butcher loaded in the same warehouse near Alicante where I last loaded for him when the whole Judas story started, though stashed in an well locked container with a forklift in front, and a well secured warehouse, overnight four thousand kilos got stolen, and this owner of that warehouse "ginger" B also turned out to have a good relationship with the Judas, and that explains where that Judas got the information from that company in Casablanca in the first place.

I believe that after these facts the butcher has largely retired, he was after all this an easy target, very good business acumen, but to soft for this business.

After everything calmed down around the theft, I was sitting one evening in a bar in Amsterdam west where I was a regular guest, at a good moment I get a call from a stranger who wants to speak with me, it was important, he said, I asked how he got my number? Wasn't that important and he would explain to me later, with this kind of anonymous strange bells, vigilance is required, these generally don't promise much good, I told where I was and soon two oversized Negro men walked in, one of them told me a man wanted to talk about the theft, i just had to let you know the time and place, "who then?" i asked, "good people" he said, i gave a location in the middle of a square surrounded by shops, and also an ABN-AMRO bank branch, it is full of cameras, besides that it was a stone's throw from my parental home, the fact that it is full of cameras was mainly the reason I passed this on as a location. The next day I was sitting on a bench in the middle of the square in question with my dog, a fila brasileiro, fifteen minutes before the agreed time, I could look around me 360^0 on the bench by moving around on the bench.

Then I saw a familiar figure on the other side, it was one of the Albanians that R had walking around him, when I looked further, I saw two more on the other side, eventually R comes up with four of them dudes, "hey how are you" asks R, "yes great" I say, and explained that vd S had kicked my cart, because I didn't see the butcher anymore, " yes, that's exactly why I wanted to talk for a moment with you"

He told me that he had dived into the whole thing in detail and my part in it was wrong "you are involved too, we know that 100%" so he said.

"Even if you know 1000%, I know I didn't made a penny on the theft period" I said

"too bad for you, but you also have to pay a fine, if that doesn't work, we know that you have a villa in Spain" then he showed the land register printout of my villa, at the same time one of the Albanians came standing intimidatingly close to me with his arms folded and said in broken English " you better start doing your best"

Then something snapped in me, me ?! who had suffered so much from the theft of another person, also had to pay?!

So I say, "Listen to me very carefully, because I'm only going to say it once, if you go on this tour I promise that next time we'll all be on the front page of the national newspaper, and honestly I don't care who stays standing or who will lay down" and i walked away, followed by the same Albanian, I stepped in my car and he even pulled on my door so i couldn't close it, than my dog tried to grab him, she didn't give a f#£&k about anything on the street, but the car and house were her domain, i told the Albanian to let go off my door or let her go loose on him, he let loose and i drove away.

When I came home upset my daughter noticed that and asked what was going on, I told in a nutshell that some figures were trying to extort me and that vd S was involved, vd S a name she heard all to often the last few months, I also told that this happened on the mall square around the corner, then she panicked and said "but mommy is at the mall!!""take me to mommy now, quick!" "Ok, ok" I say, and I think shit, those grave bins are still there, so on the way out I grab my gun and also a folding umbrella that I put in a plastic bag, and drove back at a mad speed, and yes they were all standing in the middle of the square talking to my wife on top of that, they all saw me coming and I parked like a madman half over the sidewalk while my daughter was already running to her mother I got out and took the bag with umbrellas in it and held the umbrellas by the lever and of course they never expected me to come back and certainly after what i said combined with that bag in my hand they put it all on a fast pace in the opposite direction.

In the following months I was asked by several people about the details of the theft, known and unknown, their questions and answers confirmed my suspicion, all were acquaintances of vd S, and all of them had business interests with vd S in the past, and when I told the story in a nutshell some said *"ok, thank you, then I know enough"* or *"that explains a lot of what happened in the past"* and there was someone who said *"now I know exactly where that bag with £ sterling has gone from under the sink"*, also one where a truck of stolen laptops had disappeared, so actually stolen twice, another who told me that he lost trade in England with vd S as a partner, vd S showed official paperwork about the loss, but turned out much later to be falsified process reports, A case even where 4200 kilos got stolen and for which someone has been summoned to give an explanation who was later found tortured to death in a garbage container along the highway, later turned out he had nothing to with the theft

All these cases had one resemblance, namely vd S was very closely involved in each and every one. that there have been doubts all that time by all these individuals was clear, but in some kind of way vd S managed to keep his blazon "clean" and went in great lengths to achieve that, and I knew, I had experienced that all too well, but that clean blazon of vd S laid now in shambles since that theft on the 21-8-2007

Further worth noting that vd S had the unloading location info from most likely E, the same E who tampered the butcher and ripped him off four million, E had this information from our employee P who had the warehouse in his name, this P turned out to make extra income by letting several people unload hash behind our backs, including E, the info about the company in Casablanca came from "ginger" B, and that's how this whole debacle arose, I've never seen vd S again, reportedly lives in Dubai now, there are more going there that are on lists to be removed from the game what I hear, very strict gun laws there, hoping karma catches up with vd S the Judas, I wouldn't shed a tear, yes of pure joy.

" Blame it all on the death"

During a detention in the infamous "bijlmerbajes" in
Amsterdam I met a number of members of the Etienne U
gang in the yard, including the not unknown Bert C and a
certain Sammi S, S had a Canadian passport and was of
Jewish Lebanese descent, the gentlemen were in for a large-
scale hashish trade to a variety of countries among them
Canada and Scandinavia, S was a small man of maybe 1.65
with clearly Jewish appearances, he looked like two drops of
water like the Jewish mayor of Amsterdam Ed van Thijn, he
told me that he lived in southern Spain with a woman of
Moroccan descent with whom he had a child and despite that
he had Canadian nationality, he had also lived in Sweden for
years before that, coincidentally, among other things, the
countries the gang were accused of having smuggled to.

I became quite good friends with Sammi, he even moved at
one point to the wing where I was detained, the man was a
wizard with his kettle, despite the fact that these - as the name

says - are only for boiling water- the man made all kinds of dishes in it, but because of his cooking skills the wing stood

"The infamous Bijlmer jail"

completely blue every now and then, also he had to buy a new kettle every two weeks

My detention did not last very long and Sammi had to stay for another year or so.

Visited him after his detention near Malaga where he lived in a villa in Benalmadena, flew regularly up and down and became more and more friends with him and eventually even bought a villa through him in the street where he lived, further it occurred to me that even though he had previously worked with a large hashish organization he didn't have a nail to scratch his ass, [skinned] drove a ford focus that was falling apart from misery, always and everywhere I paid the tapas and the glasses of wine, I even lent him 4000 euros on a Persian carpet that he left as a deposit, and also tried to join forces to earn some money, Sami what i already knew had many contacts in Scandinavia and Canada and after asking around with my contacts In the end, a number of meetings took place in Marbella with a few Moroccans and a Dutch organization, the plan was eventually to send 4 to 5 tons with a sailboat from Morocco to Canada where the merchandise would be distributed by contacts of sammi, as soon as the trade had landed I would receive 20 euros per kilo for the introduction. Sammi was going to Morocco to find the right hash that was suitable for the Canadian market, I was happy with the deal, I like those kinds of adventures and thought I would also go to Morocco for an adventure and some extra dough, , but it turned out completely different afterwards, behind my back sammi had put a condition on the table with my mates, he reasoned because my good friend cees houtman had just been murdered, sammi suggested that maybe i could be in the spotlight of the police , so it was better that I didn't go to Morocco, up to that point I understood it, but he didn't want me to hear anything about, among other things, time and locations, in fact I wasn't allowed to know anything at all, I was a "liability" he had said, it really made me sick, but because the Canadian market is one of the most lucrative markets in the world my buddies wanted to take the deal at all costs   so they urged me to agree, what I eventually reluctantly did,

What convinced me was that my Dutch/Moroccan contacts guaranteed me that once the stuff was safe in Canada they would inform me immediately and pay me. I didn't hear from sammi for a few months and my friendship with him of course was moderated, but it got much worse because in the small village where we lived where there was a lot of talk I had received information that sammi on top of the 10,000 euros and the central air conditioning that I had installed in his villa for the introduction and purchase of my current villa that he had also earned a considerable amount by playing a theater piece in collaboration with the real estate agent basically together they had given the impression that there was another candidate for the villa, because of this detail I knew that the info had to be correct because this incident had indeed taken place, and because he knew that I wanted the villa he had increased the price to a price that I did not want to pay at first, so by Sammi my "friend" i paid way too much for the villa that went straight into his pocket, "dirty little rat" i said to myself i was totally total not charmed by this action of that little f☆^*khead, and later also ventilated this to my Dutch contacts who had entered the Canada story, they pressured me not to slap that sammi or even say anything about it to him, they told me that they were now at an advanced stage in the adventure and had invested a very substantial amount, an amount that would run into the many millions, once the items arrived in Canada. Not long after my "friend" Sammi rang the bell and saw in my camera that the man was driving a brand new BMW 5 series, I let him in and I greeted him, I tried to appear as normal as possible but I can remember that this really took some effort, the man was very happy, was wearing all brand new clothes and a way too big louis Vuitton bag on his shoulder, or maybe he was too small for the bag, looked weird anyway, also he was wearing his golden Rolex, a watch he hadn't worn since he was out of detention because the strap and the timepiece were broken, in short it could be seen that he was in a good slump.

"nice wheels" I said to him..

"Yeah, I have to sell it for a friend" was his reply, of course I thought, that's the oldest B.S excuse in the book.

Completely happy he started to give a monologue " you can pick up your bit of money, i fixed everything, the gear is on the other side" Canada] then he started quite pleased with himself - say walking next to his shoes - to tell a whole story how good he really was, and that without him this would never have been possible, it was in a manner of speaking that he harvested the hash himself had beaten, pressed, brought to shore on his bicycle and swam to the sailboat with the trade on his back, I listened and looked at the man and it made me sick all over, then came the most beautiful thing, his Persian carpet lay in my living room under one of my tables and as he continued to ramble on about how good he was he walked across the carpet I had loaned him $4,000 earlier on, he looks down and says..." oh yeah, the carpet, well i give you your money back on it, but not 4000, i mean i brought you people a super story in Canada, i think i give you half of the money"

I was boiling with rage by now, such a good friend as he was in jail but what a filthy sneaky rat he turned out to be in real life.

I think before this goes wrong I better tell I have to go because I have an appointment or something because I was totally eating myself so I said I had to get out the door right away Once he's gone I went into my backyard and had a blast with the ax on the firewood yelling "DIRTY LITTLE MOTHER FUCKER!!!!!" how I had come to hate this man.... Unbelievable

Shortly afterwards I flew to Amsterdam to meet the people of the Dutch organization to finally hear the true story and to receive my money.

We agreed on our regular spot, a large restaurant near the Amstel station, they showed themselves happy so to speak, the boat turned out to be loaded with 4.2 tons of hashish 30 miles off the coast of Morocco at the height of Larache, from there the boat had sailed to nova scotia, a deserted coastline of Canada where it was unloaded again 100 miles offshore by a Canadian fishing boat, the captain and crew of the sailboat and that of the fishing boat still had to be paid and the stuff was stored for the time being in a town of Truro , not a gram had been sold because Truro was still a little less then 2000 km from the final destination Toronto. But as promised they could at least give me half of my money the next day. I agreed and then told about my last meeting with Sammi, and of course also told that despite the man never had a euro in his pocket, it now showed that he had money, this surprised them, " we have paid him like 20,000 euros expenses during the time he was working in Morocco" said one of them, I asked what he had actually done there in Morocco, the story was that he approved the trade, not even everything, and that most of the trade was delivered by the Moroccans of my friends, and about 1.5 tons through contacts of sammi, this money was delivered to sammi in morocco, this was about 475,000 euros, then I felt there was something wrong, so I say.."according to you he hasn't earned a dollar yet but the man looks and has an attitude like he has tons" and again they urged me to keep quiet and not talk about anything with him. After a few days I received my share and flew back to Spain. I really ate myself inside over that Sammi, luckily the man had moved from our street to the other side of the village, but still very close to my house, besides that the village was so small the chances were that you can run into each other several times on the same day. Which of course happened because not long after that I was sitting on a terrace and saw him with his wife and child standing in front of the traffic light in his new BMW (which he had to sell for a friend), he saw me too and was even shocked when he saw me, he laughed like a peasant with toothache and gestured that he would park and he would be with me on the terrace in 5 minutes.

I nodded with a straight face that that was okay.

A little later he came over with his wife and son, what I immediately noticed that he was very emaciated and that he looked very bad.

Very "coldly" I said goodbye to them all and he started to talk a little nervously about his general health, "I am not doing well" he started, I agreed that I could see that and asked what was going on, he told me that it started as a testicular inflammation but despite antibiotics the pain and swelling did not go away, he had appointments for second and even third opinions with various specialists, he had heard of one that it was certainly not a testicular infection, but this doctor didn't knew what it was, he went back soon for a puncture then he would definitely know what was going on.

The whole crying story and the pathetic look in the man's eyes made me kinda push the anger and all the bullshit he'd been up and what I think was coming to the side, and with a very frugal smile I told him and his family goodbye and hoped not to see him for a while.

A week or two later I received a message that one of those guys from the Dutch organization would come by to talk to me and sammi and if he could sleep with me that one day that he would stay at the costa.. I agreed and as a bonus I would pick him up from the airport.

Shortly afterwards I picked up my buddy and the fun didn't really splash from his face "I need to have a good conversation with you and sammi, because things are not right" ...me "what the heck?" he told me never not 4200 kg had arrived in canada but something more like 3800 and that the crew got 33.3% of the trade instead of the 25% he had assumed, to think on top of that the crew of the canadian fishing boat also got 10% he said, so he had already lost 43.3% of the trade before even a euro was earned, and in fact more than 50% because of the 400 missing kilos, and then he didn't even mention all the extra costs in morocco, which made the average price of each kilo already exponentially high. And because the discussions between the crew of the sailboat took place with sammi there-so he said-he has to consult with us.

"But mate why do I have to sit there, I can drink that man's blood, he has sidetracked me with your consent, I mean I feel partly responsible, and I would like to assist you, but I don't want have anything to do with that sammi."

I also said that it became clear to me why he did not want me as a snooper in Morocco, he wanted to have his hands free that became clear, I started to get an idea how he had paid for that BMW.

The next day there was a meeting between my buddy and sammi where I wasn't even around, later my mate said that sammi thought it was weird that I wasn't there, even asked if I was angry or something? So apparently the rat at least had a good mind because he had hit the nail on the head, my friend was not interested much in my story, only thing he was interested in why almost 400 kilos were missing because he knew by now that most of those kilos were missing from that part of that 1500 kg that sammi had bought, and why the crew of the sailboat had taken 33.3% instead of 25%, on both questions sammi had answered evasively or at least negatively, he did not know, it had to be right stories , everything was right when he delivered the stuff in Morocco blah blah and the crew as far as he knew should have taken 25%, he got nothing further. My buddy didn't hit him too hard verbally spoken, because he felt sorry for him because he did look bad and sammi informed him that they had found a tumor in his testicle, they just didn't know yet whether it was good or evil tumor.

In the end because of the beautiful weather, my buddy stayed for a few more days and finally some good news came, the first payment from Canada had arrived, it was a little more than 700,000 euros, which was less than 15% of the total amount, so peanuts, was by far not even enough for the purchase price of the products in Morocco.

After my buddy flew back to the Netherlands, I went into the "nightlife" of the village, and met a good acquaintance of mine and sammi, who again told me a nasty surprise, he told me that sammi and his wife were very condescending about me, this person even told me that they said I was a big drug kingpin, here!? In that small village where everyone knows everyone! i almost exploded, i wanted to drive straight to his house but had promised to hold back for my dutch friends, i knew this man who told me this would definitely contact sammi, so decided to use him as a messenger, i had to not even asked him to get the message across, it would surely happen anyway, then i thought about how i was going to formulate it without talking about 4 tons of hashish to Canada of course, so i told this man all about how and where I got to know him, about the poverty he lived in, the deal with the villa, the Persian rug, everything… and every sentence I started with "that filthy filthy rat", made an impression because the man's mouth dropped open in surprise , I concluded: "Unfortunately I can't kick the shit out of him because we have mutual friends who don't want that, but believe me testicular tumor or not, I slap him like a bitch with all the love in the world"

The message got through that was 100%, it had to be seen how he would react….not so, ..I normally saw him every day through the village with his son who was taken to and from school, but I did not see him anymore, not 1 week, not 2, it seemed like he had disappeared, moved or something, he lived 7 to 800 meters away from me as the crow flies, I could even see the roof of the complex where he lived so I went there one day took a look, and sure enough there was the BMW, completely hidden on a parking lot of a training field, which meant that the man still took his son to school on the other side of the village every day, only now he had to drive for miles to avoid me, so the message had arrived.

My Dutch friends had contacted me again and wanted me to come to Amsterdam to consult, because it was months later and apart from the 700,000 euros, not a single euro had been paid.

"with all due respect, what can I do about that?"

"I'll tell you that when you're here"

I flew to Amsterdam and met them at the usual place.

They made it clear that this couldn't go on any longer, the trade had been there for a long time, too long and the man on the spot, a certain Q who did the sales and distribution, said that it was very difficult for him to get rid of some varieties, and that therefore the the vast majority had not yet been sold.

"and then?" I say

" you were one of the first to receive your share, long before a gram was sold, we know sammi and his mates through you, we want you to take some responsibility too"

"How, do you want your money back or something?"

" no, no, we want you to fly to Montreal at our expense and there you convince yourself and therefore us that indeed most of that trade is unsold, Q is aware that you may come say to do a "check"

After some deliberation I agreed and received a blackberry phone and 2500 euros and an "anonymous" debit card with 1000 euros on it, with that blackberry I was in direct contact with Q who I had already met several times with sammi in Spain , this was in the very early stage, a big oversized dude who was expensively dressed with expensive sunglasses of Cartier or Tag heuer in short he liked the good things in life, wining and dining, golfing, nice cars and women from what I remember of our frugal conversations.

I flew to Montreal with KLM sometime in January and had prepared myself reasonably well, because I know from the "border control" program, among other things, that customs in those commonwealth countries can be a real pain in the ass, they always ask what your reasons are. so had contacted a lady in Montreal through a dating site, built up a virtual relationship so to say, emailed her that i absolutely loved her and that i wanted to meet her in person, built up a lot of data about my planned departure with her and had bought a ticket.

Wasn't really needed in the end because I just walked straight through the costumes, I took a taxi to a hotel near the old port of Montreal, and it was ice and ice cold that city in January, once I was settled in my room I got the blackberry turned it on and contacted Q.

He quickly sent me a message that he could see me in the restaurant Swartz, which turned out to be one of the oldest and most famous Jewish specialty sandwich shops in Montreal. Took a taxi and once there I have rarely seen such a thriving sandwich shop in my life, people standing in long lines waiting for their sandwich in the freezing cold.

When I messaged Q that I was on site, Q messaged me back that he was on his way and that in the meantime I should try a smoked meat sandwich, Swartz's specialty.

Indeed impressive that sandwich, Q came in with some angry looking what seemed to be some kind of bodyguards, he came to sit at my table and shook my hand, his two bull terriers stood at an appropriate distance.

"what the fuck is going on mate?" I say

"nothing, slow, just slow" he said

I asked him if it was the material? or was the market full? were there better and cheaper products on the market?

He said that was not the case, there were just varieties that sold very difficult, I asked if he knew what I was doing there 11 hours flying from Amsterdam?

"To see me?" he said laughing...

" to see yes, but not you.." and I gestured as if I were smoking a joint and gestured with my index and ring finger to my eyes and pointed both at the table.

For a moment he lost his self-confidence, and with slightly dilated eyes he said, *"I need to organize that, but that doesn't make much sense anyway, most of it is in Toronto area, and some here, and the stuff here I am repressing"*

I let it sink in for a while, so the trade was and in Toronto and in Montreal and what was here in Montreal was in the reprint press.

I asked him how much is here, and how much is in Toronto?

He shrugged, *"don't know from the back of my head"* was his reply.

I told him I came with a mission, I wanted to visit both places and see how much there was.,

The way he looked clearly it didn't bode well, irritated he started to mutter about trusting- trust story, I also told him, *"trusting is nice, controlling better"*

He told me that he would try to organize that I could take a look inside the pressing shop, but that the owner really didn't want to reveal his location at all, he didn't even know where the pressing shop was, it was easier, so to speak, to see the trade in his home city of Toronto.

But he would try to organize it, he promised me. I went back to my hotel and heard nothing that day. The next day it snowed and still no message received, irritated I sent him a message.

"Hey mate how are things going, I am not for fun here, besides hotel costs 130 CD [canadian dollar] a night."It wasn't until midday that I received a message stating that the man from the press was organizing it, but that it couldn't be done before tomorrow, and that I should be glad it was possible at all. I sent a message back that I appreciated it and if he kept me posted, so I'm aware.

I had seen in a brochure in the lobby that around the corner was one of the largest underground shopping centers in the world, 20 miles of tunnels covering 120,000 square feet.

I spent the rest of the day there, going from lunchroom to lunchroom, satisfying my shopping mania in the meantime.

Only then I suddenly think of the woman I had met on the dating site who of course knew I was in Montreal for a long time, felt stupid so went looking for an internet shop this was because for security reasons I had not included my own communication, did some searching and saw a shop with men with beards and turbans and knew that this had to be an internet shop, what it was, I opened my mail and I now had I remember well 18! Received e-mails from the lady in question, some I read, started off worried at first, then sweet, but there were some where she accused me of dating other women at the same time, to even one where she called me a bastard, I thought I make it up with her and besides that I was also curious

and decided to send her an email with an excuse why I hadn't contacted yet and an invitation for whenever she wanted.

While checking my other email I received a response from her, she was relieved and asked where I was, I sent her an email with another apology and wrote that I was in the underground shopping mall.

Immediately she sent an email that she would be in the shopping mall at an agreed place within 1 hour, I agreed and went to the place in question.

This place was maybe 5 minutes away, so I used the mean time to buy maple syrup, a typical Canadian product.

I looked at my watch and the lady must be here any moment, I was now also scouring the area for a lady in her mid-thirties, a woman of mixed race background, she had told me in her emails that her father was from Barbados and her mother was half French half Indian.

An attractive woman with some nice teeth and a smile, what I remember from the pics. At a certain moment I see a woman looking around the few terraces who somewhat matched the photos, I was on purpose somewhat hidden behind a planter and therefore she did not see me directly, I looked well, and thought, ... she don't look like in those photos.

I got up and waved at her, she looked, and yes it was her.. She hugged me and took a seat, immediately wanted to know why she hadn't heard from me for a day and a half, I didn't feel like explaining it at all, I mean it's a lie, like Friedrich Nietchze once said, you have to keep a lie simple, the more you spread out about a lie the more likely you are to get caught, so I told her it was what it was, and as distraction I asked if she didn't want anything to eat or drink. She read through the menu and I noticed that from the acrylic nails she had there were a few missing which looked like she fiddled around in an base pipe from time to time, [I remembering the nails of my sister in law who was a heavy user] and I looked at her again, and I think.....this isn't the bird from those photos from that dating site?...mixed race...yeah, ..but not at all that well-groomed look and that beautiful smile, unfortunately I couldn't look at that site or check my mail to do comparative research, after all I didn't have my phone with me and besides that we go back to 2006 , then all that did not work by a long way as it does today

I didn't need to eat anything, I had been walking from lunchroom to lunchroom all afternoon, so she ordered a steak with fries and a bottle of wine for both of us and I started to doubt her in connection with the person from the dating site,

The food was yet to come and I couldn't suppress my curiosity about her true identity so I say to her.

" do you mind when I run quickly over to the turban internet shop?!"

She looks at me with a questioning look." yeah, mm, yes go ahead"

I said I forgot something, and that I just had to check for a new email.

There was nothing strange about that in 2006, you pay mountains of roaming costs everywhere, there was hardly any wifi, and the internet did not work as it does today.

I ran to the internet shop and took a seat behind one of the screens, went to the relevant site and logged in… there she is, pictures were taken in some tropical place, really all made in a pose, almost professional. i look around to see if she happened to have run after me,..no..i scroll in...that's just not the woman at all, or it's the same one with totally photo shopped photos, or she had since the photos been full on the bottles of wine and a bit on the base pipe, I mean she didn't look like a junkie now, but she does defo look like she is on something.

I check her photos and press print and close my session, I walk to the turban and ask for my prints and the bill.

Again I look at the pictures, and try to take in details like ears, nose, eyes...well, enough fold them up and put them in my jacket.

When I arrived, her food had just been brought, and she had already drank half the bottle of wine empty

."Hi, are you okay? she asks, I said that everything was fine and excused myself again, while she ate I studied her while we did small talk.

I look at her and I think I just ask, "these pictures you send to me and the ones on the dating site, where and when were they taken?, while she chews on her steak, she thinks, and she thinks a bit more while chewing, and after she swallowed her food..."they were taken on Cuba" she says, and starts cutting off another piece of her steak. "When?" I say, frowning hard, she says…"couple years ago"

Me again." how many years ago?"

She; "Gee, are you from the police or something?"

Me; "noooo, but its just you look so different"

While she was again chewing on her food she looked straight at me in my eyes, she said nothing for like 5 seconds. Takes a toothpick, and with one hand in front of her mouth and with her other hand she fiddled around with it, then she finally says with a very cool look..." people change"

She knew I sossed her, I just knew she wasn't the woman in the pictures, and she knew I knew, and by now I knew she knew I knew that she knew I sassed her

In the meantime I laughed and asked if she would like a dessert, she said she would check the menu again and I got ready to go to the bathroom. "excuse me" I say.

I'm in the toilet and think I'm just going to tell her I have an appointment and see if I can see her tomorrow, then she never hears from me again...better, the woman is bad news, I can just feel it. I walk back to the table and from a distance I see she is not sitting at the table, I speed up the last steps to look, no gone, I look down both corridors ...nothing, I ask behind the bar to be sure, ..." the lady, you guys know where the lady went?" One of them had seen her get up and walk to the right towards the nearest exit.

Nice I thought, I'm fine with that, I put on my coat that hung over the chair and ask for the bill, only then do I feel in my pocket, ...wallet gone!!!... Then suddenly the fear creeps in my heart, i feel in all pockets, ...my blackberry gone too!!!!!!

fuck sake!!! Totally fucked I feel again through all the pockets, that bad woman totally screwed up my life for today, I explained to the staff that I couldn't pay because of theft, but told them I was in a hotel not far from there, and would pay as soon as possible, according to protocol, the mall security must be notified they said, who arrived promptly and took me to an office, I gave a verbal statement about the incident and looked at some CCTV footage, and indeed there she appears to be walking out the sliding doors, and just as I am about to get up to leave, a guy knocks on the door wearing an orange vest, they let him in, "look what I found" he says, and puts my blackberry and wallet on the table, " *in the bin just before the exit"* i look in my wallet, everything was in it except the cash, maybe 300 Canadian dollars somewhere, say 240 euros was missing, the security man explained that this happens a lot, stuff which doesn't have any value to them they dump in wastepaper baskets, I thanked them kindly and returned to my hotel after paying the restaurant bill with my card and another life lesson richer and my tail between my legs I left. Early the next day I received a message from Q asking if I could be on an outbound in an industrial estate on the outskirts of Montreal at 2:00 pm, to which I replied affirmative, thinking to myself the day before and what a gigantic headache I would have right now without that blackberry.

I went for a breakfast buffet at the hotel and studied the map of Montreal in the lobby, the industrial estate was about 18 km from the hotel, I estimated the driving time as half an hour, and my plan was to hail a taxi nearby at 01.20 and then went back to my room to relax on my bed. About 1.15 pm I went down and then hailed a taxi near by somewhere,

 [not in front of the hotel for privacy], it was snowing again, and not a little bit, probably because of that taxis didn't stop, everyone wanted a taxi with that dog weather of course. Eventually I walked back to the hotel and threw my privacy overboard and took a taxi in front of the hotel, but it was now 13:40, I gave the driver directions and asked how long it would take. "normally about 30 min, but with this weather more like 45 minutes" he said.

 Shit, I'll be half an hour late there. I thought. Once there, there was a van, a kind of A team model and a black RS6, exactly the same as I had in Spain and because the snow came pouring down from the sky I couldn't see who was in the car, the Audi flashed its lights, I made my way to the Audi, the passenger door opened and a skinny guy with a mustache got out and gestured to take his place as he got in the back.

Q was behind the wheel and two white guys in the back, one had tattoos on his hands and neck, and they said hello to me in anything but friendly manner, and the skinny guy said while he hit the back of my seat,

" is it normal where your from to let people wait for an hour?"

Q; "these are the guys of the pressing shop, they are not to happy but they take you to their location"

"I can imagine, but things need to be done" I said while I looked at the skinny guy and at the back of my seat to let him know I didn't like that much…hitting of my seat

"so Q, monkey see, monkey do?" I tell him referring that he drove the exact same car except for the interior.

"told you I liked the car" was his reply

He went on to tell me that I had to take a seat in the back of that van, so that they kept the location of the reprint shop a secret.

That didn't make me happy and asked if that couldn't be done differently, say lay in the back seat with a coat over my head.

Q then points to the GMC van and says *"than you have to first put a backseat in it"*

"Ferfucksake!" it was a GMC van with only seats in front, *"how long?"* I said

The skinny guy with the mustache said with a bored look "stop *moaning mate, get in and we go, we lost an hour already because of you!"* I again asked Q for the quantities of both locations where my friends their trade was laying.

"I'll get you them later, okay?"

I was still nowhere two days later, didn't know jack shit

I got in the back of the GMC van that had some empty boxes and some filthy blankets in it, as I fold them to sit on it, that skinny mustache slams the door, *"hey take it easy driving!!"* I yelled at him, he then hit the side of the sheet metal with a loud bang.

The bus started and off we went, it was not a very interesting trip, and everything except comfortable in the back of a dark van, besides that it was freezing cold, it took at least 35 to 40 minutes until the van drove into a garage, which I heard.

The back door opened and that skinny mustache thought he was funny by saying *"come on sweet doggiedog"*.

"your having a laugh mate" I said to him.

"follow" says the other what I did, I followed them through what appeared to be a not too small complex and ended up in the press room, several carbon filters were hanging from the ceiling for the stench, there were a number of large freezers and a hydraulic press, and obviously a big sausage maker machine.

I was familiar with this setup, I mean I pressed tons myself, and told them that too

"good for you mate" was the reply from the scruffy skinny trailer trash mustache

By now they were both sitting on a freezer smoking a cigarette and watching me.

"so where's the gear? I asked, one of them pointed to a freezer, I opened it and saw all plastic containers with a brown stuff in them, this stuff had clearly already been processed and still had to be pressed.

"how much is here? I asked, then suddenly the men started speaking French among each other. And on top of that they still owed me an answer.

I took out a container and asked if they had scales, very funny that mustache gave me a kitchen scale and laughed, then he pointed to an industrial scale in the corner and sat back on the other freezer. I couldn't get that thing on, and made a gesture for them to turn it on, very almost tired the other got off the freezer and turned it on.

It was clear that things were not going well for them, and they didn't feel like cooperate in. I realized this was a mission impossible, I couldn't identify the material, and after I weighed two of the plastic containers and they didn't even know the tare weight of the bins they told me that in all 12 bins in there were exactly the same weighed 18 kilos each

"Where's the rest? I asked, *"somewhere else"*

"this is crap boys" I told them.

Then that skinny mustache went a little loose on me

"What the fuck, don't make your problem ours, you must be happy we show you our place mate, otherwise we put you on nearest bus now!!!"

"all ok, lets wrap up, this is going nowhere, ill inform my people back home and the only one that has a problem is Q, not you guys, neither me"

"get me to the nearest bus or taxi stop and I am out of here"

This statement clearly gave them relief, they were rid of me and they were not accused of anything.

The skinny mustache stayed behind and with the tattoo boy I walked to the GMC bus, I crawled in the back of the icy GMC bus and urged him to keep the ride as short as possible, which he strangely enough with a genuine approving smile agreed with

He dropped me off behind a gas station in what I could see at first glance not the best area, I didn't care, I wanted nothing more than to be in my warm hotel room and walked into the gas station to have them call a cab .

Less than an hour later I was in my hotel room texting Q and venting my grievance about the state of affairs so far.

He messaged me that he couldn't bend iron with his hands or anything like that either, And promised to give me all the figures by noon in Jewish delicatessen Swartz

I knew this trip had been in vain and also knew that this Q was not "straight forward", he was hiding the truth, and the next day he would show me manipulated numbers, numbers that would match what he had paid up till that moment.

I would stay exactly 7 days, I had completed 4 and started preparing for the journey back.

The next day he walked into Swartz with one of his bull terriers, he put an envelope under the table in my hands and says "*there are some pictures in there yesterday taken from everything that's left*"

He told me that after this he drove straight to Toronto, according to him about a 6 hour journey by car, and wished me luck.

I didn't trust the man with that big potty body anymore what I had experienced during this trip, but was very curious what kind of pictures he had put in the envelope, so went to the toilet to take a look at them, photos yes, from kilos of hash, whether it was my friends' hash I couldn't determine, on top of that I could not determine how many kilos there were, because they were laid out in such a way that they could have been behind and under bricks, nor was there any newspaper in addition to the date clearly visible from yesterday to actually prove that the photos were from yesterday, these photos could be months old, in short, worthless.

I put each photo on the toilet piece by piece, and took the sharpest possible photo of each with the blackberry, then I did the same with the accounting, then I tore everything into small pieces and flushed it down the toilet.

I mean I'd rather not be stopped with these kind of holiday snaps in my pocket.

Everything was on Blackberry's encrypted pgp system and then put the phone in a double-zip bag with the story of the lady in the shopping mall still fresh in my mind.

It's been cold in Montreal for the last few days, but sunny, I've done some site seeing in the Old Port, and had a great time in the city.

I flew back to Amsterdam where I contacted my mates who were only too eager to see me.

We met at a snooker center on the canal where they had rented a private room with snooker table for the whole evening, they brought food and drinks and, somewhat delighted, they sat down on a chesterfield couch to "hear the good news", well that excitement quickly disappeared after I started telling my story, there was also nothing good to report, I showed them the photos and the accounting which, as I thought before, fairly corresponded with what had already been paid.

I had seen 12 containers with my own eyes each containing 18kg of brown crushed stuff, couldn't even smell anything as the stuff was frozen, all in all it was a useless trip.

Shortly afterwards I flew back to the costa del sol where I heard in the village that sammi had been hospitalized and would soon have an operation, I heard the news and it occurred to me that it did not stir any emotions in me at all, I took in the info, shrugged and said something like "oh, well, that's to bad" or something to that effect.

I didn't even ask if he'd had chemo, if it had metastasized, nothing, it just didn't interest me, the man had stepped on my soul and fucked with my head.

I went on with my life and forget about that man which was easy, because i knew some more sammies who were honest, there was always work to be done and money to be made in my world.

Another month or two later and I didn't hear much from anyone about the Canada/Sammi story, I came back from Barcelona eating at my favorite restaurant in the village when I heard that sammi had passed away, it did nothing to me.... again, I thought it was shit for his I think at that time 6 to 7 year old son, that's all.

A few weeks later I saw his wife and son just come out of the supermarket, we said hello to each other and she immediately started with a sad face that Sammi had passed away, "sorry to hear that" and then I asked if she knew what had happened between him and me, she looked at me questionably and says " sammi brought you very good biniss?"

I told her that what he had brought was far from good and that a huge amount was still outstanding, I also told her that Sammi who I thought was a real friend had hurt me, that he as a friend has left me in great disillusionment, and therefore I will not shed a tear for her husband's death.

Funnily enough, she nodded in understanding, I greeted them both very modestly, never to see them again.

Not long after that I received another message from my Dutch friends, with the request if I was in the area to contact me. No rush so I asked, "actually yes" he sent back, a few days later in Amsterdam they told me that they had received a

payment of 280,000 euros but then they had received a message that the cake was finished.

He said that he and his buddy were not satisfied with this message and couldn't make chocolate from Q's messages.

And if I wanted to fly to Toronto this time to meet Q, just for a chat, no visits to presses or stashes, just a chat.

"When?" I say,

"Fast, as soon as possible" was his reply.

I told him I wasn't itching to fly there again, I had something else to do.

Think about it, let me know soon, you'll get the same resources as last time, money, a card and a blackberry.

Shortly afterwards I informed him that I would go there again, but that this would really be the last time, he gave me the means and went to book a ticket as soon as possible.

The flights were all full, I was able to book one that left in 5 days and returned after 4 days, full fair ticket of 2300 €

I prepared myself a bit by not snagging a woman on a dating site this time, but by buying a ticket to an opera gala and a ticket 2 days later to visit the Niagara water falls, all the relevant information i put it in a plastic folder together with my hotel and ticket booking, all in all a package close to 3000 € I boarded a packed plane full of seniors Dutch who had already booked group trips a year ago, during the trip I was in between such a group and most had not even paid more than 300 € for their tickets from what I heard from some old lady's sitting next to me.

The seat belt light was on and Toronto was only a 20 minute flight away, it was early morning and could catch a glimpse of Toronto with its CN tower, one of the tallest towers in the world, I also had the tower on my bucket list, a skywalk at 450 meters height .

We landed and I went with my hand luggage to the costumes area, when I arrived there I could walk right up to the exit where a man in civilian clothes and a name sign asked if I was traveling alone, which I confirmed, "in that case you have go back and answer some questions" he says, pointing to two rows.

Once it was my turn, I was confronted by an obese, clearly authoritarian black woman, apparently to get straight to the point, she asked me why I was traveling alone?

"Because I'm divorced and living alone, that's why," I say.

Wasn't a satisfactory answer for the somewhat surly woman.

"You are trying to say that people who are divorced always travel alone?"

I shrugged and said "well this divorced man travels alone"

"what kind of business do you do sir, and can I see your booking of and ticket and hotel?"

"of course" I say and look for the folder with papers in my travel suitcase,

"Well?" she says very impatiently while I was on my knees, I get up from my knees again with the transparent folder in my hands and look at her like….what?

" again sir, what kind of work you do?"

I told that I had a share in, among other things, a clothing store in Amsterdam, and that I had a portfolio in real estate.

"Which clothes store in Amsterdam?" " can we look it up on internet? Let me look what time it is in Amsterdam, mmm..can we call this store? Do they know your name?"

I think WTF, what a fat bitch this woman is , meanwhile she was looking through my bookings.

"I see you bought a very expensive ticket, who paid for this ticket?"

"me" I say,

she "cash or credit card?" the answer was actually cash from a travel agency, but i said i bought it from a travel agency with my credit card, i knew they couldn't possibly verify this.

She then says "you've got all the right answers don't you?"

"do you have any cash on you for this trip?"

" yeah, about 500 euros, and a card for emergencies "

" are you planning to spend this 500 during these 4 days you are here?"

"I guess so"

" so sir, lets resume now, you come for four days to canada, spend on a ticket, hotel, and some entertainment 3000 euros, on top of that you plan to spend 500 and some of your card?, so in total 3500 euro for four days, you must be a very rich man!"

" no, not rich, what is rich? I am giving myself a treat"

" sir I have enough reasons to believe that your visit to Canada is not genuine and I have to ask if you step out of the line and you will be picked up shortly by some colleagues of mine" she points to a corner behind her counter and says , "take all your belongings and wait there"

Two gentlemen of the costumes took me to the back of an office and asked if I could open my suitcase, which I did and each item of clothing was examined in detail.

Then they asked me to empty my pockets and hand over my coat, and then they had not 1, not 2, but 3 phones of mine on the table and my pre-pay debit card which wasn't in my name, my paracetamol tablets were taken for examination, they said.

Then suddenly that obese Jamaican came in again, she was clearly the manager and she enjoyed asking people annoying questions "explain me, why you have three phones" isn't one enough? "

" one is Dutch, one Spanish, and one for work" I say.

" nice to know you are such a busy man, tell me which is Dutch, which is Spanish and which is for work? And could you unblock all three please?"

I told what was what and decoded the blackberry and my Spanish phone, the battery of the Dutch one was empty.

There was nothing to be seen on the Spanish, and the blackberry had, in addition to the normal standard encryption, an extra security via the pgp app, I hoped they didn't realize that, but they sossed this within 2 minutes, the fat dark woman was notified about the app by one of the two employees and he then handed the phone to her, "ok sir, now you have to understand one thing, ill point you out an app on your phone, you are not allowed to touch your phone, the only thing you are allowed is to give me the code to enter that app, written or verbally",

She showed me the app at an appropriate distance, and of course it was the pgp app, "and?" she says.

"that won't happen, that's private" I say.

She looks at me seriously, rubs her face, and says, "private mm?"

"yes" I say,

" you know what, maybe you have some private pedophile pictures hidden in that app"

We don't like that in Canada"

"I am not a pedophile and there are no pedophile pictures on there"

"well we don't know that, do we? because you refuse to give us the code"

In the meantime, I saw them take all three phones to the back She looked through my stuff and asked in whose name the pre-pay debit card was.

I told her I got it from a lady friend but actually didn't even know in who's name it was.

"Yeah sure Mr business man" then she threw the card in my travel suitcase and mumbled that my visit to the opera and the Niagara falls probably wasn't going ahead, and she walked to the back. After about 10 minutes they came back with my phones taken apart [batteries and SIM cards loose in a transparent bag], she says "I am going to ask you one more time, you going to give us that code or not?" when you don't give us the code ill declare you an unwanted person in

Canada, and you go from here to a immigration detention center and the first available flight back home"

"and when I give you the code you let me in?" I say.

She looks at me with an ambiguous smile and says nothing,

"sounds like no, so no code"

" ok prepare the paperwork for this gentleman and let him sign, than bring him to the center"

" I am done with you, don't forget to sign, as long as you don't sign you stay in the immigration detention center, but one thing for sure you wont come into Canada"

When she walked away she said it was only for this trip, if I wanted to come next month or year I was welcome, I started laughing and said there wasn't a hair on my head that would even think about coming back I told her that I don't even want to fly over Canada anymore.

A little later I received a document which I signed and was taken to that particular immigration detention center where all colorful figures were looking very apishly at a number of television screens. I settled in two free seats and would leave with a flight back to Amsterdam for which I had to wait just under 8 hours. After some dozing in my seats I was picked up by two uniformed machine gun armed men to be taken to the plane, they ordered me to walk ahead of them and we walked into the packed gate of the plane in question, completely loaded with the same kind tourists as the outward flight, they all looked at me when I was escorted by the two armed men to the counter where my ticket was ready, and then as the very first passenger I was led into the trunk, one of the gentlemen asked my seat number and both went with me on the plane to my seat, He pointed to my seat and said "now buckle up and don't leave that seat until the plane is in the air"

Then both left..

Not long after that, all the Dutch tourist crowds came in, and they really all, one by one, gaped at me, in their eyes I must have been some sort of bin Laden, or at least a murderer.

I really didn't like that they were all staring at me like that, so at a good moment when an older couple looked at me very shocked I got up looked at them and that alone made them jump back, than I put on the gorilla pose, and imitated a gorilla as best as possible with of course a gorilla scream, those poor people almost crawled under the seats. Immediately a flight attendant came and called me to order.

"What happened?" she asked

After explaining to her that this was all about a - although encrypted - app, she also had to laugh and she decided to calm the mood a bit among the people, especially those who took a seat close to me to reassure people via the intercom in 3 languages that I was harmless.

Via de intercom she said; " everybody saw the gentleman brought in by armed guards just before the flight, this gentleman is not a murderer or terrorist, the Canadian authorities denied him access because he has an encrypted program on his computer that couldn't be opened by the authorities, apparently this is not a crime in Canada but enough reason for not admitting you In the country"

She had done well, immediately a completely different mood , people around me wanted to start a conversation, and everyone gave a nod in agreement or when I looked at them they shook his or her head, like "it's too crazy for words"

After an even 2 hours longer flight than the outward journey I arrived at Schiphol completely shattered, and after a day of rest I sent a message to my Dutch friends that I was back "what?! Are you back already?!" I sent a message that things had gone very differently than planned. The next day I saw my Dutch friends who were accompanied by a Moroccan lady F, I had known this lady for years, she also turned out to be an investor in this Canada debacle. I told them broadly what had happened and advised them to be very careful with that BlackBerry because they had taken it back and removed the SIM card. They were all sick of it, one said "damn this shit, you flew to Canada twice, cost a total of 7 k for the cat's cunt"

I wasn't happy about it either and said that I would never go again and that Q really had to come here now. They agreed and would urge Q to explain where the 6 million Canadian dollars were. I flew back to Spain and then heard nothing for several months, I had actually already forgotten the whole story until I received a message that Q would be in Amsterdam next week and I had to be there.

That said, I bought a ticket and we agreed again in the Restaurant where it all started near the Amstel station, there they was a whole delegation, 3 representatives of the Dutch organization, the Moroccan lady F. and two other Moroccan gentlemen, I took a seat between them and heard that Q would be there in half an hour. We drank coffee and went through the strategy regarding the questions, "I'm prepared" says one of the Dutchmen and took the lead and put a list of questions on the table for Q

But he wasn't the only one, and I bluffed him with an even bigger list that I put on the table. After some consultation, we had to wait for Q, we all kept an eye on the entrance and yes there he came, as always expensive brand clothing and expensive glasses from the brand Cartier or Porsche design, and he actually brought his two pit bulls all the way from Canada.

They came in and because this restaurant in question is a large restaurant, probably one of the largest in Amsterdam and we were sitting in the back, I walked over to them to guide them to the table.

Once at the table we all said hello and even before the conversation started there was already tension, because there were several at the table who were not charmed by those two pit bulls, one of which was completely covered with stickers. [Tattoos]

Whether those guys couldn't take a seat at the bar, or better wait outside, Q agreed and sent them to the bar.

The conversations started and everyone had serious faces.

" it is one big massive fuckup Q" said one of the Dutch.

Q pouted his lips nodded a yes and shrugged, body language that reflected exactly how he looked at it, the pout to indicate "well, but what can I do about it", the frugal yes and slightly to the side turning his head that he partly agreed, shrugging was "but I'm not guilty"

He was bombarded with questions about the story from start to finish, about my first visit to Montreal and why I didn't saw anything. Until even one of the diners accused him outright of maintaining a very luxurious lifestyle at the expense of all those genes at the table.

" no, no not true, totally not true" he said, the man remained very calm and took a number of A4s from his pocket full of calculations.

Since he didn't have copies for everyone, my two mates sat around him and studied the calculations.

I knew these had been totally manipulated and sat at the other end of the table and didn't bother even looking at them.

I still saw my friend do his best to understand them or perhaps to catch him in some malformation. In very fast Dutch so that Q didn't understand I said "all shit man, leave it"

To every question Q had an answer ready so that he got away unscathed. He had to take one verbal blow after another, he gave the impression that it really touched him, but inside I knew he was laughing, after all it was him who would walk away as the big winner

This man had prepared this theater piece very well, he had made it his masterpiece, and he didn't had to fear nothing, we were in a full restaurant and the two pit bulls kept a close eye on him It was about the sailboat and the percentage that was still in dispute, the blame was placed on the captain who, like Sammi, had also died.

And when he was cornered, he reluctantly admitted that things could have been done differently.

But there was one who really had to pay for it in his eyes, Sammi, Sammi was blamed for almost everything that went wrong, of course there is nothing more beautiful than blaming everything on a dead person.

Every time he mentioned his name.." I don't want to blame Sammi, may he be in heaven, but it was him who… blah blah

That guy made me feel sick and I forgot my question list so
I only said one thing;

" you know Q, I am wondering how someone who is in
charge can fuck up such a beautiful story, a story that goes
straight from a producing country morocco to the most
lucrative market in the world Canada, when you did this right
and you repeat it several times a year we all could be multi
millionaires in no time, we did our part, we got it on your
doorstep, from the moment it was on your doorstep everything
went tits up, in all our eyes you are a messer"

"there is more to it, you guys weren't there" he replied

"that's exactly the problem" said one of the others.

"You can say what you want and blame everything on dead
people" said another

It looked as if the man had a plate in front of his head, it was
noticeable to me at least, that if he would squeeze his way
through this and then the road ahead was smooth for him, he
had shown his best side had explained "everything" and that
was it, and then he flew back to Canada, a million or so
richer.

And that's exactly what happened, not long after that the conversation ended and no hands were shaken and besides Q nobody even said goodbye, it was final, the 6 million Canadian dollars or the 4 million euros would never ever be paid.

Sadly enough one of the Dutch men that day present from what I heard later invested all of savings into this story, he even had sold his very valuable antique comic book collection to pay other investors who were putting a lot of pressure on him and because he was convinced that the money one day would be paid by Q, he had satisfied some of them with his own money.

Not long after he died in a council house broke and in misery

"Brain Membrane Pollinator"

You don't just become addicted so to speak from one day to the next, although I've heard that methamphetamine users become instantly addicted.

Often it is a progressive steady process that develops over months but most likely years, different for each individual.

 In our stores half the regular clientele snorted, every now and then I tried some, and the cozy me was gone, just didn't feel comfortable, I can remember an incident somewhere in the summer in an attic of an Australian lady, her boyfriend at the time was a very good friend of mine and who also present, the ex wife of Charles G., the well-known sex shop boss, and a chubby German, we were all full of booze and the German was in possession of 1 or actually 2 bags of

"von das beste material", of the best material, we were all reasonable pissed sitting at the kitchen table from the Australian lady and drinking a bottle of Remy XIII, or something of that caliber, my mate loved that stuff. And the German was busy with a plate full of lines, thick and thin, your choice, "diese ist fur dich" this one is for you he says, and pointing to a thin one, "du bist anfanger", you are a beginner, there I went nnnnnniff...in one nostril, and hop another where there was still room left, bwahhhhh, straight into the brain membrane, bang, bang boom, again that uncomfortable feeling took away the cozy loose feeling of the alcohol, i immediately tell my buddy that I'm not really feeling good, and asked for large bottle of water from the lady of the house, I also went to rinse my nose in the sink, but it was too late, it had already largely penetrated the brain membrane.

For all of them I was the one who spoiled their party, that big oversized guy who was complaining that he wasn't feeling well and took swigs from a big bottle of water like it was the last one on the planet, after a while the lady of the house offered me

262

to lay down on the sofa in the living room which was divided with glass and leaded doors which I gratefully made use of, she closed the doors and I just hope that messy feeling soon end, just as I was trying to go to sleep, suddenly that fat sweating German sits next to me, with his plate of devils dust, he says, "don't you want to try from the other bag, one is Bolivian and is much better than the other Peruvian you had before, much more relaxed", he said, it really took me a while before I could convince the man that stuff and I didn't go well together, ok he says " ruch an, slaf gut" , [sleep well] that didn't really work out either, only by the time the sun came up, and because non stop talking from them i put wet toilet paper in my ears, man they did talk , and glass leaded doors didn't provide any sound proof either, I think I woke up around noon, I could still hear them talking, pulled the plugs out of my ears and looked over my shoulder they were still sitting at the same dining table, loft hung full of smoke, and I went eavesdropping, Boy, what stories everyone had, nobody listens to each other, all nonsense stories and one cut the other off in the middle of his or her own monologue to start with their own monologue, really about nothing, meanwhile the chalices were still being filled and also the nostrils, I think I'm going to have a cup of coffee in the neighborhood and take a taxi home, open the glass doors... "Good morning!, or afternoon actually", I say, and it was

263

freeping hot under that roof, "why don't you guys open a window? "and they all looked at me with those weird pupils, white, almost grey faces, and a few had foamy white spit in the corners of their lips " better not , for the neighbors" said one of them, probably paranoia i thought, and say "I wish you guys a nice productive day and leave", with my experience over the years i know it's impossible to stay around people who are pollinating the membrane, unless you are pollinated yourself, I called my buddy a few days later, they had continued until late at night the next day, he than spent 3 days in his bed after that.

I kept my distance to that stuff and that remained until sometime around the year 2000, when exactly the "spark" hit me is hard to say. I had always been a visitor of brothels, knew them all in the city and far beyond, because we also made "excursions" to well-known brothels as far as the province of Limburg.

"DON'T CAST YOUR PEARLS BEFORE SWINE"

"DO NOT GIVE WHAT IS HOLY TO THE DOGS; NOR CAST YOUR PEARLS BEFORE SWINE, LEST THEY TRAMPLE THEM UNDER THEIR FEET, AND TURN AND TEAR YOU IN PIECES" **(Matthew 7:6)**.

But it all started to change when i discovered the combination between sex, alcohol, and other substances like coke, ecstasy, poppers, this combination made me loose all my boundaries, and this must be one of the first time the spark hit me, in the luxury brothel Golden Key Club in the center where I was a regular guest, and for anyone who was a regular in this establishment around that time they probably remembered the two sisters, mixed race, beautiful bronzed girls, long legs, massive facades , easy cup E, my favorites, these girls were often occupied, one was a bit bolder than the other, once I was inside the somewhat cheeky sister was available, I followed her up the narrow staircase , once undressed i admired her body for a moment.....than she says " we going to make it a very horny night "and she took out a pack of coke which she empty's out on her make-up mirror and starts chopping, I say, girl that's doesn't work for me, takes away the fun, she says "don't mend to be funny at all, we're not in a bar, you're in a whorehouse! It has to be horny! She holds the mirror to my face with cut straw, "for you" , 2 big lines , nifffff&naffffff there It went. While she stands in front of me going threw her bag, "try this", she says and she took out of her bag a little brown glass bottle with a red yellow sticker on it, she closes with a finger one of my nostrils and holds the bottle to the other, I sniff., "and now the other", poppers they call that stuff, then I went on a space trip, than she sits on my lap and she pushes my face between those big boobs of hers, looks at me and says, "you have enough money with you? I could barely talk I was spacing that much, "yeah like 3 or 4 grand or something, she pouts her mouth a bit, and says mmmm, credit cards? Yes, I say, visibly satisfied she gently grabs my nose and says, "well mister this is going to be a very expensive night" Not to go into all the details, one thing I did for sure, I licked like a lassie dog, had a dick the size of an anaconda in my head, but nothing bigger than a north sea shrimp between my legs. you give in, everything is so horny, so beautiful, your deepest perverse feelings come floating up.

This was clearly a trick she used before with clients, You pay normally by the hour, but the hours were more like 40 minutes, one after the other bottles of Moet champagne got brought in, then her sister joined in, and on top of everything the so called "present" the coke also had to be paid , 80 per gram, times 5 = 400 so in a few hours i was threw my cash, all took until about 7 or 8 in the morning, though i was completely of my skull I was not that much off an baboon that I noticed they emptied the glasses of Moet in the bubble bath, around 7:00 am without a thank you but extremely happy both ladies left the room leaving me on that big bed which had a big mirror above it, there I lay, wallet empty, alone, paranoid with eyes the size of a shit fly, the manager offered to let me recuperate before I went out on the street, but for 100 per hour, so that card went through the machine again, it's clear when you are in a state like this everybody takes the piss, by noon I dared to go out on the street again, not even a minute of sleep, I really had to go, they wanted to close the place, door opened and immediately got almost knocked over by a cyclist, I felt like shit, I had the feeling that the whole world was looking at me and thought, "Look at that dud", once home I immediately crawled into my basement, afterwards I received a nice bank statement of 4350, so i had spent 8000 in one night. Still, I somehow found it "nice/horny" because I had been in that room with those 2 ladies for about 6 to 7 hours, it's a miracle I didn't have calluses on my tongue.

Whether this is absolutely the first time I don't remember, but certainly one of many, unfortunately there would be 100s of nights and days, because sometimes i stayed away for 3 days at a time , were these ladies to blame? I don't think so, they didn't hold a pistol to my head

But they surely were the facilitators in my movie, even so I alone was responsible for the decisions I made, or was I? Once on that gear I was totally out of my mind, did anything to continue a session, would have robbed my own mum . Did this happen every few days? not really, this "acting out" as they call it between sex addicts.

This "only" happened every few weeks till the money ran out that day and of course physically and mentally drained, then recuperate, and the cycle started all over again.

Licking my wounds, and sometimes I would isolate myself for days, avoid my wife who was anything but stupid and who quickly realized that her guy had a huge problem so slowly but surely, I realized that I was my own worst enemy.

All over Amsterdam in clubs and red-light districts I held my sessions, one thing I never did was take my own devil's dust with me, so my preference were brothels and prostitutes who had the stuff, at one point I was so well known in the red light district that the Dominican prostitutes who worked there at night all called me the " aspirador " or the vacuum cleaner, because I sniffed easy 5, 6 or 7 grams in a long session. When I came to some clubs the ladies would be jumping and arguing to see who could get me in their room first.

And in the clubs i just loved the attention i got from the lady's, they all wondered around me, i felt like a movie star, maybe it was because the attention i lacked when I was a kid and they knew I was good for it, they all knew i was smashing thousands a night so I was super interesting for the ladies. Amsterdam has three red light districts, two in the center and one in the south of Amsterdam and I have like a million footsteps in each one of them, the attraction was enormous for me, no barriers in terms of time, after all they were open 24 hours a day at the time, they were within easy reach, I was in each within ten minutes in the nightly hours, only barrier was parking, but of course I parked my car right on a bridge and took it for granted that my car got towed away, when I was in my movie I didn't care anymore.

In the red-light districts the red carpet went out, if I walked around there the jungle drum went around quickly, ladies who's doors I knocked on and if the curtains were closed, which means they are occupied, pulled me in and put me on their bathrooms and than kick out their client as quickly as possible. But the jungle drum went around even faster when my money ran out, no more curtains opened. When I was under the influence of the "marching powder" and walked with a wallet full of money I felt like Charlie in the chocolate factory, all of the woman looked so beautiful in them red lights, but when my money was gone and I would leave my watch or my phone or both to carried on. And of course, never thinking about the consequences and the hangover. And even though I already had paid thousands, I soberly went looking the next day for the lady in question where I had left my belongings, and sometimes i was shocked to death, then It was no longer Charlie in the chocolate factory, but more like Johnny in the haunted house, Had I really spent that much money on that monstrous woman? The night before she looked like she came straight out of a Playboy.

Clearly sober in daylight completely different story. There were also some downright diabolical women, stealing, lots of stealing, pushing you to smoke a crack pipe. At a certain point the sessions became more and more frequent, and once I was spacing out till all my money was gone than I started calling my mates to bring me money, as at that moment I was still good for it, I owned a big clothing store in the center, and so every now and then I had the contents of the cash register brought to me, really now that I write it down, it's to crazy for words, I was completely undressing myself financially, and I kept it not exactly a secret by calling my mates and staff in the early morning hours usually to hand over money to taxis or to those prostitutes, probably with a voice that sounded more like some weird Mongol. This calling to mates has a much bigger negative side effect, which actually costs a lot more, the world in general but especially I was in it's not that important what you can do, the most important thing is your reliability, you obtain reliability very slowly, they say reliability comes on the back of a turtle and disappears on the back of a racehorse. Once the whole city knew I was walking from one whorehouse to the next leaving thousands of euros behind it became increasingly quiet with work.

As the sessions got longer and longer and I started consuming more and more the Charlie in the chocolate factory feeling turned in total paranoia which wasn't exactly fun for the ladies either, especially if they had taken all your money and they were stuck with a snorting skinned madman in their loft who refused to leave, because I didn't dare to go out on the street anymore. I was convinced that my wife and children were waiting on the corner, it was total madness, the police came regularly. I remember one time I had already been busy with a session for 36 hours Then scored some more money and was invited to finish my movie or session as you like with a Ghanaian "lady" who lived in a building in the South of the city with a few lady friends, once there I laid a pile of money down, but I had no more devils dust, " no worry's, i have" the easy virtue lady said and she puts some of that junk on the table, not powder more like a rock and when she pressed on it with a card the rock actually shattered, i knew it was something unusual but that didn't matter to me, it was white, and there were lines made out of it, I snorted it, my God not even caring what it was, I sat down and all the lady's looked almost afraid at me, one even said *"you look like you are possessed by the devil"* i don't know what happened next, but i do know i had a total blackout which must have lasted for minutes, because i only came to my senses when standing with a chair in my hands that I was just about to throw through a window, I look around, I had smashed everything to pieces, with my bare feet in the glass, blood on my feet, no one else was in the apartment, looked outside, saw 2 police vehicles, and there were like 15 pedestrians looking up, including the ladies in bathrobes, then I heard on the stairs ... POLICE!! POLICE!! , with guns drawn they came in and told me to lay down, i apologized that i had blacked out, they were wary keeping their hands on their holsters and asked me to get dressed, i asked them if I could put a shirt over my head to avoid the whole charade., they handcuffed me and there I went to the police station. Once there they called a doctor for me and asked how the hell I could have gone that crazy, after examination the doctor gave me a soothing pill, and after drinking a few liters of water they let me go, the lady in question had not filed a report, not so strange, after all those retarded amounts of money I had left behind in the past.

I've ended up in intensive care 3 times, and I mean intensive care, not emergency care, if you add those times, maybe ended up in the hospital a total of 15 times.

Also that time I had been on it for 18 straight hours , came home, lay down on the couch, felt extremely restless, felt my heart pounding like mad, tried to count my pulse, tick tick tick tick tick, uncountable that quickly, got more and more restless, stood in front of the mirror and I looked terrible, bloodshot eyes, deep in their sockets, dark rims under my eyes, but more disturbingly my nail beds were purple, this brought me in panic , god knows what kind of shit these whores had given me? , sometimes they have nothing themselves and they started to call street dealers, I thought to myself, what the hell you snorted? Maybe it's finely chopped heart medicine you've stuffed up your nose.

All these thoughts and those purple nails made me decide to call an ambulance

After consultation with an 112 employee who asked if I could still walk, and in that case, advised me to call a taxi and go on my own to the nearest hospital as soon as possible. Taxi stopped in front of my house and the taxi driver even looked worried, "hospital I hear from central?" Yep, and fast!

Once I walked into the emergency room, I saw young football players sitting with their mums in the waiting room with either a leg up or some other injurie, of course I drew their attention when I was at the desk, they looked like "look at that dud", it's fun to look at such a snorted clown, much more fun than a boring waiting room.

There was no way I was going to sit in amongst that crowd, but the nurse who worked behind the desk saw that I was not doing well at all, so she indicated that I could walk threw the Electric door in to the emergency room, there a nurse received me and asked me to sit down on a bed behind a curtain, than she asks me what I had used and took my blood pressure and heart rate, and after seeing the results she told her colleague who was now half looking through the curtain, "Call the cardiologist immediately and ask if she can come here urgently!" This announcement made me even more agitated than I already was, I was seriously terrified now. Shortly afterwards a fiery lady came who looked worried, she asked the nurses on duty a few things, without hesitating she said: "directly to the I.C., cardiology department!"

I was rushed there on a stretcher, once there I had to sit on a bed with a number of monitors behind it and my whole body was covered with wires which were connected to those monitors, I also received an IV with a thick needle in my arm and some pills of which one I had to dissolve under my tongue, the cardiologist seemed genuinely concerned she stayed with me all the time until everything was installed, she asked me to try to relax," we've given you something soothing, and you'll be here under observation for 24 hours."

I actually felt a bit calmer, and the fact that I was in good hands also helped me to relax.

Later that night, or maybe it was only hours later turning in my sleep and a detector went loose, a high-pitched alarm went off, and a nurse immediately came in to re attach The next day when blood tests showed that I had not suffered any lasting damage from raping my body and i was on the point to being discharged from the hospital, the same cardiologist came walking over and made gesture i had to wait, she turned a chair in reverse direction and took a seat, than she said, *"Listen to me very carefully what I have to say to you, you came in here 24 hours ago , you were lying on a stretcher, well not really lying, you were kicking your feet, throwing your arms around, clenching your fists, in short totally a-relaxed, now the medical cardiology aspect, you came in with values, such as heart rate, blood pressure of someone who was running a marathon, and*

that while lying on a stretcher, your blood pressure was 158
218, we assumed that you would have a heart attack at any
moment, your blood also showed that your glucose level was
that low that a coma was one of the possibilities, furthermore
we found something I have rarely seen, we found an enzyme in
your blood which showed that you were out of your direct
energy reserves, you were using your muscle mass as an
energy source, they call it catabolysis, something that you only
encounter in people who climb the mount Everest

Catabolysis is a biological process in which the body
breaks down fat and muscle tissue in order to stay alive.
Catabolysis occurs only when there is no longer any
source of protein, carbohydrate, or vitamin nourishment
feeding all body systems; it is the most severe type of
malnutrition.

Source:Wikipedia

All in all you are in your early 40s with the heart of a horse, a
strong constitution, but sir I can give you on a note what will
happen if you continue with this, there are two outcomes
possible, the death or the geraniums, and by that I mean an
acute heart attack, you just getting older, not younger, the older
the greater the risk, and the geraniums, by which I mean you

will have a brain hemorrhage because your blood vessels can no longer handle the pressure , then you will be unable to talk and end up in a nursing home for the rest of your life sitting there dribbling spit from the corner of your mouth, do you want that, Mr. S? Do you really want that? Now the medical aspect, there are three medical prognoses, because something bad will happen, either a heart attack, a brain hemorrhage or you blow your kidneys to shreds" Then emotionally she said If you love yourself stop this self-destruction, now, get help, today, you are worth it. did it help? yeah, a few weeks maybe... I've experienced these kind of life-threatening self-destruction stories all too often, how long has this nonsense gone on? Long, way too long, how much did it cost??? A lot, to much, I've got an idea, but its just to embarrassing for words and not to mention all the negative spin back, the stupidity, the thefts, because you attract a lot of nasty people. The way i behaved doesn't garner you any respect, you have to command respect, which certainly doesn't happen if you call your mates in the middle of the night or early morning to bring a few thousand, or to you're staff to hand over the contents of the till to a bunch of lady's of easy virtue, during these sessions you treat yourself and these women like shit, and the same treatment you'll get in return, its a giving fact that if you act like an imbecile, people will treat you like you are one. Besides that, what happens

277

when you really get a heart attack in such a place, most of these characters wouldn't care less, they make first sure your really dead and than steal what you got left and only than call an ambulance. Really only once during all this acting out in my life I remember one lady who showed some empathy, when I got a bleeding nose she tried to stop the bleeding with some tissue paper and while she did that she looked me in my eyes in a worried way and suddenly tears run from her eyes , and said " Please, please stop, change your life, you are going to die"

But most of them couldn't care less, I experienced it more than once that in my house stuff had been stolen, escorts also have boyfriends who are usually not the kind of duds who have a 9 to 5 jobs or going to work with a lunch box, i met over the years in our bars in the red light many dudes who had their spouse or girlfriend working behind the window, in the beginning as a young kid i couldn't wrap my head around how the hell you can let your girlfriend or wife have sex with one unknown man for money, let alone, having sex with twenty men or more on a single day, over the years i saw some of these dudes dropping their spouses off and guiding them to a window, and at the end of the day picking them up again, some even them stayed all day around "to show her that he cared "and in the mean time witnessing one man after the other having a piece of your wife, many couples like that came to drink a beer or smoke a spliff in one of our bars after the female side had been working, and believe me they looked and behaved like normal couples, almost like they genuinely even loved each other, i got to know some of those couples well over the years and noticed these men not only have dominant characters but are real manipulators, very sophisticated they give the girl the impression they are in a totally normal relation and do a normal job.

I remember one couple which the dude often said when they left " come on girl we have to go home, tomorrow another working day" than I wondered how he copes with that, once home having dinner together and after watching hand in hand a romantic movie on the couch, romantic kissing knowing your girl gave head to a platoon of men and the most astonishing having sex with the woman from who you know she had sex all day with all kind of men in all different positions imaginable, like nothing happened, these men or must be very big selfish narcissists or total sociopaths or both, of course i know they are pimps in disguise, some of these duds I've seen over the years with different lady's, so when the previous relation broke up, or maybe the girl in question left because she realized what matrix she was living in.

Spoke in two occasions with girls who broke up with such a dude, both of them the same tragic story, one girl I knew very well, and I met her "boyfriend" in a few occasions, she was a regular client in our bar, and i was a regular client at hers, she came in sad one day and asked me to go out for dinner together, during the dinner i noticed she needed to get something from her shoulders, she told me that she had broke up with her "boyfriend" recently, " he left me with nothing" she said with tears in her eyes, of course i wanted to hear the whole story, so i let her do the talk, apparently shortly after she met him he persuaded her to work as a prostitute, "how?" i asked, because i am interested how these guys operate in an otherwise very sophisticated way, as she said, after living together for a month or so, he started complaining that he could barely pay the bills and that there was almost no work, and she was completely in love with him had to go back to her mother so he said, and that they had better end the relationship due to lack of money, she was devastated, a few hours later he "suddenly"[totally planned of course] had the solution, he had a friend whose girlfriend earned a lot of easy money, and there they had to go to visit for a chat, and there she was so manipulated by him and the couple that they went to buy lingerie the next day and she was working behind the window the same evening, she was only seventeen, than the plan was the money "they" made "they" would invest in real estate and he recently started building a villa in Portugal and the money she generated every week which she than had to transfer to Portugal, she even showed me a whole bunch of copy's of the transfers, and when i took a quick glance at them, all six, seven some even more than ten thousand, he even had asked if she could please start working six days a week, and work over the weekends double shifts because he had a deadline constructing the villa, he always told her whatever "they" made was from them together, the plan was that once the villa was ready they move to Portugal and start a family. Than the girl started to cry, and said " I've got nothing anymore, he took it all", what a bastard i thought and asked her how much he embezzled from her, she didn't really know, but she said "we've been over five years together, and except for a holiday so now and than i worked non stop 5 sometimes 6 days a week" i gave all the money to him, only kept money for food and clothes", so how much you think? I said, " maybe a half million" she said with tears in her eyes, well i wasn't exactly green behind my ears, i knew what girls made in them days behind the window, a good looking girl made easy thousand a day, and this girl was extremely good looking, she worked on the other side of the canal from our bar, her curtain was always closed, i mean i was a client myself from her, i remember in even in one occasion when i visited her and once ready she kept the curtain closed and said "i want to finish my cigarette for a change" always she had man wondering in front of her window, sometimes she even had bus loads of tourist in front of her window admiring her, she was one of the absolute crackers in the red light, so i calculated quickly from my head, she makes minimum 20.000 a month, times 12, and times 5 years, is more like one and half million she raked in, minus food and clothes, this girl had made the man a millionaire, , i didn't say this out loud to her, not in the state she was at that moment, i did say " i think it could be a bit more" without giving more attention to the subject, than she says, he even stole her Porsche 911 , which he embezzled the documents from and quickly switched ownership.

Now she had to start from scratch she said, and indeed i saw her rent out her body for a few more years more But I have to admit I didn't mind that much.

I knew another girl who had opened a safety box under the ABN AMRO bank on the dam squire, she did this together with her boyfriend, the pimp in disguise he had told her to put all her earnings in that safety box because it was "safe" there, she trusted him she said, they even had a three year old son together and he was always so nice to her, and because it was that long ago she had even forgotten he had signed for the safety box also, until they had a fight about really nothing she said, it was about such a futile thing that she thought like he staged it even, when she came back from work the house was empty and a bit later she found out the safe to, " how much was in it?" I asked, she didn't respond, to embarrassing I guess, must have been a lot because she looked devastated. Left alone with his kid without money, disgraceful dog of a person After i saw that pimp boy friend from the girl of the Porsche once in our bar and couldn't resist asking something about the state of affairs, so i said, "hey i talked to your ex girlfriend, are you proud of yourself now?" or something along those lines, i remember very well his answer because it was an astonishing one, he said, " she shouldn't complain so much beside that i learned her a trade" Some of these dudes after they sucked one girl dry they just start looking for another pray where they continue to parasite on, after a while I sassed it all out, and when i saw these cunts with yet another pray, I felled the strong need to in some kind of way or form to warn these girls, which is again very tricky, because some of these pimps in disguise aint easy boys, but when i had a chance and they were alone in our bar i would say " hey you heard about that girl who drove that Porsche that works on the other side?" and i told them the story, and let them self put the puzzle together without me getting in harms way, all these kind of men, well you cant even call them men, characters who maneuver young woman into prostitution by manipulation with the only objective to steel their money are disgusting human beings., not even worth the oxygen they breath.

Most of these pimps in disguise provide their " girlfriends" also of drugs if needed whether its for them or for their clients and they always look in any way shape or form where they can cheat steel and embezzle more money so i had once again spaced out of my skull a few of these lady's at home , i ordered from one of these lady's some more devils dust, she said "no problem, my boyfriend could bring if you want" i agreed, so when he called her to notify he was in front of the door she ran to the front door to grab a pack of devils dust and than what i noticed later she deliberately didn't let the door fall into the lock, and because i lived in a three story apartment the girls kept me busy on one side while they ransacked my house on the other side without me noticing it, i only noticed after they left, all electronics were gone, hi fi installation, clothes etcetera, in hindsight this could have created of course very dangerous situations, uninvited guests while you yourself walk around completely sniffed up paranoid through that same house, that's a recipe for murder and manslaughter. Fortunately, it never came to that, but it could have easily happened. Somehow, despite the fact that I had a massive addiction, money continued to be made, I still had the confidence of a number of Moroccans, and because I was already in Spain a lot at the time, I had set up a logistics network from there to the Netherlands, plus storage and distribution, and as I said before I was not on the run day in and day out with devils dust, I also always remained faithful to my gym, participated in organized running 10 km, and I joint several times the Dutch champion ships indoor rowing in the Apollohal, i rowed the 1 km in 2.54, and the 5 km in 15.38, according to members of the NA this most likely saved my life, with that 1 km rowing I pumped my heart in rest from 65 to over 200 beats per minute within 2 minutes. And of course there were friends who warned me about my self destruction I had a friend where I used to buy my wife and my cars from who was concerned when he heard once again that i was lying in a brothel for a few nights giving my money away like old newspapers, but was it for my health or because I maybe couldn't buy anymore cars of him? What I like to emphasize saying this, when you are an addict, people even some of your best friends become opportunists.

He made an appointment for me with an owner of a rehab clinic, my mate told me that he was the best in the field. I took this with a grind of salt because i already found out with previous encounters with problematic abuse of substance guru's that there are many scammers in the addiction industry who abuse the desperate position that the addict and their family are in. After the introductory talk in a fancy hotel, I was invited by him to the headquarters in Barneveld, luxury place with high end cars in front of the door, once sitting in his office the owner told me he had exactly the same problem as me, sniffing and whorehouses, only he was regularly carried away from those places on a stretcher, he said, could be true or could be nonsense, however it was visible that the man had somewhere during his life a serious problem with nicotine and alcohol

He told me that before he started in the addiction business that he was busy in the marketing world, was notable too, smooth sales man talk, he guaranteed me to cure my addiction in no time, which is of course a blatant lie, nobody can cure your addiction except you and your believe in an higher power. He was in contact with clinics all over the world, 30 days internally for 1000 eu per day, I thanked him for that, he also had clinics for 15,000 per month, I agreed to go in therapy and massages, more than 7000 eu i paid was x times psychotherapy and x times massage, came to 70 eu per session, really helped zero. Over the years I must have spend tens of thousands on treatments, clinics, psycho therapy, you name it, nothing helped. I don't want to generalize entrepreneurs in the addiction industry, some of them are honest people who really want to make a difference in somebody's else's life after where they themselves went threw, because after all most people in this business know exactly where you are coming from.

But all these clinics do is beside taking your money they are giving you tools which might change you, but again that's totally up to you if you use those tools.

Its your addiction, and believe me it will always stay in a dormant way with you, in addiction circles we compare it with a monkey you carry around on your shoulder, most of the time the monkey is quiet, but its there, even if you go to the north pole, when you feed the monkey alcohol, and spiritually there is lack on positive input this monkey will tab you on your shoulder, and its up to you if you let the demons in, so an addiction is a constant struggle to find balance. And its really there, i know guys who were clean 8, 10 even 12 year, and they end up between "friends" in a neighborhood where they consumed mind altering stuff in the past and they surrender to the monkey, and go on a session of a week non stop consuming.

I don't want anybody to feel hopeless reading this, but you have to be aware, vigilant, always remember where you came from. When you are a daily consumer your body is totally poisoned, so what most clinics do is first a period of detox so you have you're brains on the right spot again, there are some who use Burundanga or Ayhuasca as a treatment, these are natural parts of plants that grow in south America and Africa, these treatments are very potent, you go basically on a total trip, that's why while treated there must be by law always a medical professional present, some say that they met their creator during these trips, others say they made a trip threw the galaxy, others had a chat with their ancestors from the 16th century, i don't know because i never did it, but i do have some positive feed back, apparently the trip is so heavy that it resets your mind so to speak.

Stopping drinking minimized the chance, but If I filled myself with beer or very rarely though without beer, but with a few thousand in my pocket, I'd just be playing Charlie in the chocolate factory again.

There is saying which men often say to each other after a few beers in a playful manner and when they are for example in the middle of a divorce or have their spouse moaning for money

"Every woman is a prostitute except you're and my mum" but *about your mum I've got my doubts"* and no you don't find this quote under the ordinary ones like *"Love is the flower you've got to let grow."* please take this saying lightly and of course there are always exceptions to the rule, but what I mean to say is that no woman wants a looser, no matter how attractive he may be, I mean there is not something like an ugly rich man, the fact is that hardly any woman is waiting for a handsome postman who can barely keep his head above water but prefers probably an older fat guy with a bit of charisma and lots of money and when he is even good looking that's an extra.

Fact is even if you have the tiniest dick in the world but a big fat bank account, women will idolize your dick, they'll probably pretend like it's the biggest in the universe There will definitely be some who think this is a disgusting cliché macho statement, but I'm sure most men would agree with me and secretly even the vast majority of women, though they'll never would admit it publicly. Most woman are looking for economic security without even realizing it, a man with money and or power has for many woman a "sex" appeal

Going back to the Dutch saying, there have been times when was out in the disco or nightclub, I was so horribly horny after a few lines, and my pockets full of money, that I visually scoured the bar/nightclub and looked around for specific women, giving a drink, having a chat, and than asked discreetly while showing a bundle of money if they didn't wanted to go to the toilet with me for only oral sex, giving or taking, I didn't care

You will be surprised which women do what for what, of course over the years I had developed a "nose" for certain woman, and some woman agreed immediately, maybe doubt about the situation in the restroom, but just go for it, than there are the ones who agree, but want to go to a hotel or their apartment, and the ones who want to know the ins and outs, especially how much money, how long, what to expect sexually and after having satisfying answers asked your number, point is I wanted it than here and now, no bullshitting around, but about the ones who asked more info than you actually already know that they will be soon at your door in a nightgown, and then there are the ones who say simply " get the f#*^>k away crazy motherf#^*☆r!!", but many go for it ...fact!

Looking back everything was going quite well in my life until I began to consume, due all the bad decisions I made with my pollinated membrane slowly but surely everything slipped out my of hands, I had quite a port folio real estate which would have a value of around six million at the time of writing , and now i got nothing, and all roads lead back to my addiction, did seven year in prison, at least 4 are direct or indirectly the consequence of consuming devils dust. Fact is when you are an addict and you don't change, you will end up with nothing and nobody, because everybody will eventually walk away from you, including your family, in short you will lead a very lonely miserable life, because after all who wants a person who has problems with substance abuse? nobody, when i look back how I behaved during my marriage I would never have tolerated that the other way around, the only relations which are sustainable when you are an addict is when you're spouse is an addict to, so two addicts together, in that case I wish you good luck, because you need it.

"*ANOMYNOUS SEX*"

When my ex wife indicated that her patience was running out, I went to an NA meeting for the first time, there I learned to listen to others for a change, and I did understand step one from the twelve step program, that i was powerless over my addiction, and that it made my life unmanageable , if you don't see this first step, the rest is in vain, you can go to the most expensive clinics, makes no sense at all, wasted money. During those meetings at the NA I met interesting people, members of NA are often entrepreneurs, artists, people who hold executive positions in business, i did notice that they are usually people with certain character traits, not all of them of course, but many of them have dominant personalities, often they know better so to speak, and in that concern i belonged there to, but also people who have interesting lives, at the AA you come across all kinds of people, carpenters, car mechanics, housewives, I also visited the SLAA, Sex Love Anonymous Addiction, you can't just join them, you have to be introduced by an existing member, then threw say a ballot committee, after that you are welcomed, this because they have been infiltrated in the past by reporters, but even more so because people joint for the simple reason to get laid, apparently sex addicts are interesting for many. Why did I attend all these different meetings? Simply because I couldn't put my finger on my problem, was it the alcohol? which I also enjoyed quite normally, was it the coke? I only used that stuff in sex houses, never ever in a say a social way, but what was it that turned me into a perverted twisted madman who was only too happy to pay a lot extra to put the biggest dildo in all kinds of gaping orifices?

I recognized step one anyway, I couldn't control that fetish, it couldn't go on like this anymore, for everyone that recognition moment is different, for some after a few times you have felt sick to death from a hangover, for the other when you employer threatens to fire you or your spouse puts you on the street, and for another it is when he wakes up in a cardboard box under a bridge and realizes that all he has got left is that box, others are fine with that box as long as they have their drug of choice, in general it's a long and hard battle to say no to a drink or anything your addicted to, change comes mostly threw a life changing experience or a spiritual awakening. In life it is very important that you can trust your loved ones, your friends, and of course your family, but the one you should trust the most is the one you have to hang out with 24/7, that is, yourself, if you can't trust yourself anymore there is no end nor beginning in site.

I attended a total of hundreds of meetings at both NA, and AA but those at the SLAA were short lived, after I was referred by a regular member, I was given the go-ahead and they would welcome me to the next meeting, this one was fairly close, in a church about 18 kilometers away from me.

That can be cycled by me, so I went to the meeting with a racing bike including cycling shorts, shirt and helmet, once there, there were surprisingly predominantly women present. Took a seat and introduced myself, these meetings are exactly the same as the AA and NA, everyone reads one step from the

12 steps, it is also emphasized that everything is based on anonymity, everything that is said is considered to stay there, while sharing one can talk about emotions, triggers that lead to most very damaging sexual behavior, continuous cheating, always falling for the wrong man or woman, allowing people to abuse you, but it is not allowed to talk about how deep or how many dildos you put in gaping cavities, or how many hoses are emptied, all of minor importance, a meeting lasts one hour and immediately after the meeting the moderator took me into the hall and says "sir, could you please change your pants for the next time, some female members find your pants offensive, "*of course*" I say, no problem, and continue to the toilet and look in the mirror to take a good look at my pants, well, there is a sort of pad in the pants, so that the saddle does not hurt you, and indeed it pushes up the chimes and clapper a little and makes it easy to imagine the content. was not allowed anymore, another male member had to laugh, he said that he noticed when I got up to go to the bathroom some of the female members looked slightly obsessed at my bike pants contents.

Visited some of these meetings, listened to the sharing and shared myself, while sharing from others i found out i was way not the only one with my problem, I concluded that once you have the taste of it, sex in combination with drugs, all sex after is boring, I remember one dude saying that there is no better sex than sex on methamphetamine, gives all sorts, anybody with an unconventional approach of sex visited the meetings, not they talk about their actually act but after a few meetings listening to certain individuals things start to fall in place, also there were dudes attending meetings who got a kick out of flashing their genitals unexpectedly to by-passers, and one lady who I only saw three times at a meeting maybe, a bit of a gothic type, asked me after a meeting to join her for a coffee, which I did, after a bit of chatting she told me that she loved BDSM sex, after some more talking she basically loved it when men during sex to beat the living shit out of her," no limits" she said even lifted her shirt and proudly showed me her bruising from her previous sessions, this kind of talk is of course impossible in just a bar with just a man, but because we were both sex addicts our conversation was a "bit" more liberal, she told me she had a specially decorated room in her house for those sessions, if I wanted to come and take a look one day?! Sounded tempting for a moment, coz i do like that freaky stuff, but as the conversation continued, she pointed out how deep a man could put his arm up her rear end, I than thought, uff, that must look more like a stretched saddlebag down there so maybe not such a good idea after all, wasn't my kind of type anyway. By the way she pointed above her elbow. It became now clear that not only by gossip that there was interaction between members, it confirmed once more, your vibe attracts your tribe.

One of the members became a good friend of mine he had the exact same problem as me devils' dust and easy virtue lady's, A big Scottish dude, a real character, we went out for dinner every now and then and one night he was drinking heavily and i know for someone with an addiction that's skating on thin ice when you fill yourself up with alcohol, so i say "you're not going to call me to save you tomorrow morning, are you?" "no chum don't worry" you guessed it, at around 7 am my phone rang, I look at the display, it's him, fuck, what am i supposed to do with this? let the phone ring a few times, but it kept ringing, so eventually I pick up, with a totally freaked out voice" hey, it's me, please come and get me?" He was in a private house and his cash was gone and his credit card somehow didn't work, gee I thought where I have I heard that before...not to happy I told him ill pick him up , once there and the door is opened by a kind of Brigit Bardot type when she was in her fifties she said hello and told me he was the last client and if I please could take him with me, once inside i see him sitting on the couch totally freaked out, I could barely understand him, I told the woman she had to give us some time because I couldn't take him out on the street in the state he was, although with a sauerkraut face she agreed and she said she give us half an hour. I asked her for a big bottle water for him to drink so he could flush that shit through his system, she gave me a bottle and i sat down next to him on the couch and persuaded him to drink as much as water as possible and not to take any more of that crap, then my eye falls on a large kind of attaché case on the table, "from whose is that?" I ask, with a weary look he points to himself, "what's in it then?, he makes a gesture -like look in it, I open it, and there are all pairs of glasses in it, ladies models, two layers, at least 50 pair glasses, pointy frames, round frames, modern, 70s models, you name it, all tastes, I look at him with raised shoulders, like what the fuck is this? he mumbles something like, "I just like it".. I look at the woman sitting behind the bar who was eavesdropping our conversation, "he's been a regular with us for years and he always takes his briefcase with him, we know him as the briefcase man, "oh I didn't know he was in the eyewear business?" I said, then she gestures to me to come closer which I did while I urge my mate to drink more water. once at the bar she says "yeah you know that's his thing he lets those girls put their hair up and then they have to put on different pairs of glasses ..," me: well and then?" - "Well apparently he likes the strict school professor type" .. I look at her in a way that I don't quite understand, ok nice I say, and then? well then does his thing so to say and she makes a pulling movement with her hand. This really had to sink in for moment, I looked at him and see him spacing on the sofa, i thought

WTF! I couldn't help it and i started laughing like I haven't done in a long time and yell at him "hey mister speck saver!!" you ejaculate over pairs of glasses?!" he didn't know where to look, I was really glad I had picked him up now, I haven't had a laugh like this in ages, once he looked acceptable i took him home and all the way I just couldn't stop laughing while Mr the optician speck saver still looking like he was of his skull sitting next to me with his fancy attaché suitcase on his lap, unforgettable.

After i came home i felt shit for the man, and was sorry that had laughed that much, i mean i went so many times threw were he went threw that night, its all so sad, your money gone, card blocked, feeling like shit for days from all the alcohol an that devils dust you put in your body, i thought it would be appropriate to offer my apologies to the man-which i did-, apologies accepted, and he didn't see any problem in my laughing, on the contrary, it was a lesson for him, it showed him yet again that once he started with the dust that his demons revealed.

From some lady's, in particular one i didn't quite understand her problem, was a single mum and a total nymphomaniac, nothing wrong with that I thought, a sexually active lady, did not use drugs, did not throw thousands of euros out the window, in my eyes no problem, so i had a burning question for her, or actually due to over the years my twisted perception of sex more an advice maybe, I never said anything to her, just didn't have the opportunity up till than, but when we decided to go to an Italian restaurant after the meeting with some members I saw my chance.

I sat next to her at the table so I could have a private chat, and believe me my choice of words had been carefully considered, after talking about small things I thought it was time to the build up to the key question.."with all respect, but if I listen to you, you're sexually very active, though with different partners, but, but I mean, it's not that serious, is it?" she didn't look amused at all, shook her head and said "you know i don't understand your problem either, you go drinking knowing you might sniff and then you end up in a brothel where you leave all your money behind!?" Simple solution, just stop drinking, problem solved! I don't understand that again! Uffff, I had clearly hit a nerve "you know" she says, I live in C. and do my shopping in F, which is at least a 20 km drive, just like you I act out, every few weeks, I do that, it satisfies something in me, then I rest, then it accumulates until it hits again, and I let myself abuse in a ridiculous way by just some man whose name I don't even know. She said this in such a serious tone that I almost felt intimidated, she was clearly offended that I didn't see her problem. So very carefully I continued, *sorry but may I ask how?*

How? she replies, "*When I go shopping and I see a guy I like, I go to the same shelves and look for something that wasn't even on my list, make eye contact, this first eye contact usually says everything, for example there was a guy with a work outfit (plumber,) , I had a cart full, he got 3 articles, I see him checkout, I leave my full cart for what it is, and walk after him at an appropriate distance to his van and call him with an excuse that i have a problem with a sink or something that keeps coming back, 10 minutes later I'm fucking in the back of his van between the plastic pipes and the tool boxes And of course, not with every guy i can do this, but i just try, is part of my addiction, the excitement around it all, sometimes I go to a gas station, deflate my tire and call a guy I like and say I don't know how to inflate my tire and make some flattering comments and fuck with that guy the same day, maybe fuck the same guy*

4 or 5 times, until the fun is over, and then it starts all over again.

That's why I'm driving 40 km for a carton of milk and a few slices of cheese, sir! I do this because I can't control myself, problem is at the supermarket around the corner from where I live I do the exact same thing, but than everyone in the neighborhood knows what a filthy slut I am, and I have kids like you, mine are 6 and 8, what if they are 16 and 18 and they hear that their mother is getting fucked by all kind of men in vans on the parking lot of the local supermarket? That's my problem sir, can you understand it now maybe!? "Yes, I understand" ..or maybe i didn't, of course I walked around the red light district for years, and also knew some prostitutes who were total nymphomaniacs, and believe me I just wanted to help the woman, I had the feeling that I had the best solution for her, so I guess I'll just say it, but, "*why don't flip it around, and make the problem into something that benefits you?,* or something to that effect, she turns her head slowly towards me, looks at me with an almost devastating disapproving look, she takes the last zip of her coffee and puts the cup back on the saucer with a bang, and yells " *FUCKING MEN!*" that bang of the cup and "fuckin man" was enough to get everyone's attention at the table, the lady got up without saying goodbye to anyone and walked pontifically to the exit. No one had heard of our conversation, but they all looked at me like: what the hell did you say to that woman? My friend D took me aside, " what happened man?!" Well, long story, but in short, I asked her why she didn't go and work as a prostitute? "You did what?!" he yells as he throws his head to the back between his shoulders. Oooo ferfucksake Everett, why did you say something like that?! That's a total insult man!! He ran outside but the lady in question was already gone, and as he came back said "I don't know man, but this is off the scale!

That was my last meeting at the S.L.A.A ever, I never went back.

D. did make the offer to come back, but on the condition that I would apologize to the lady, "ok" I said, "but could the lady also answer my question? "He looked hopelessly at me and said; " you are a fucking nutter mate"

The use of cocaine can cause some very perverted feelings, this is especially the first hours, unfortunately after years you also use larger doses, and no doubt that horny feeling will turn into total paranoia.

At some point you are on a high, higher isn't possible, if you continue to consume, a change can take place, I could suddenly have had enough and think to myself " what am I doing here"? Or if I was at home "what are these people doing here"? Of course, I did know what they came for, but I suddenly just wanted to get them out

Sometimes I called one or two escorts, who call depending on how much money i still had call 1, 2 or 3 more, so sometimes i had 5 of those characters walking through my house, and god does not know who they are, so when i had that aha moment I noticed there was a woman with a dick walking through my house, or depending on how you look at it, a guy with tits, that's how I once also had one with breasts and vagina, just complete woman you would say, but in the morning light the "lady" walked through my house with a stubble beard and I even had to call my tenant" Hank de trucker" RIP to kick that converted guy out, it didn't wanted to go, had also consumed itself, was also paranoid, and in mean time hank almost pissed his pants laughing, this character was completely converted but had a bit of a Gordon Brown syndrome, needed to shave twice a day, The growth was so heavy that it could not be controlled with all the hormones in the world, it was a real haunted house, it took at least 2 hours to get ghost Gordon out, it is also from this kind of Gordons that you get weird viruses. I also experienced the strangest things during my "dildo and tongue" sessions , was already busy with a session for 8 hours and of course money was gone and I was totally paranoia, the "ladies" in question wanted me to leave, but I was far from "ready" to go, then one of them called her boyfriend or pimp after some threats, not long after there was a banging on the door downstairs and I hear a few guys screaming, making me totally paranoid , so paranoid I almost begged the girl not to open the door, but when the banging didn't stop and the girl made it clear to go downstairs i took the stairs to the attic, away from everything, *no no she says, not there!!* I saw no other way out, so I just went up those stairs, I eventually end up in a messy dark attic.

(in the red light district, buildings above windows are usually not rented out, not practical, and enough rental income from prostitution) meanwhile I have two prostitutes after me who shouted that I had to come back, I see a small skylight and climb through it, as it was dark, the prostitutes stood at the bottom of the fleece stairs screaming at a safe distance from that totally mad, snorted nutcase I climb out the window totally paranoid, walk over the roof tiles to get what I saw on a flat roof further on, and the last meters through yes a gutter! to walk, ten meters high through an old zinc gutter, and those women screaming behind me through that skylight UTTERLY INSANE!!!! With all the luck in the world I end up on that flat roof, couldn't go anywhere, where to now? All I wanted was to be as far away as possible from those women and those pimps whose voices I could hear from the window, everything went through my head, maybe there were neighbors who maybe have called the police by now, I was on a roof of about 8 by 4, bordering on two sides by walls and one side a patio of say 3 by 4 meters and down there were windows visible from three floors when i looked down I saw a small tree and a table with a few chairs, on the other side was a much larger flat roof and that's where i decided to go, in the meantime I hear those women and those pimps take turns yelling, so you don't believe it, and I don't either actually , but I quickly take in the situation, I walk back as far as possible from that patio against the wall and get ready to take a sprint to…..to... jump over that patio!!!! I somehow had the wild plan in my head to run from the narrow side so a 4 meter sprint I wanted to jump over a 3 meter wide patio that was about 10 meters deep, take a sprint stance, waited a moment, still looking, clear moment i think to myself….this is impossible , looked down at that table and chairs, it was actually scary deep, i felt like a rat in a corner than suddenly i see to my right a few small colored lights, walked there and i

306

see a door with a window i look inside I see that these lights are from a refrigerator, I feel the handle, open!!! And suddenly i am in someone's kitchen, see shoes neatly lined up, I open the next door, I enter the hallway, quietly walk down a staircase to the front door, open it and get back on the main canal, 2 buildings from that alley where it all started, I walk to the left among a couple of other pedestrians "as if nothing had happened", a few minutes before I almost died, smashed to death on someone's garden furniture.   Years later I got confronted in an ugly nasty way with one of those idiotically imbecilic   precious nights, 27 k , I sat on the train from Amsterdam to the north, I looked outside and at suddenly i hear Hey, Oe Oe, I look towards the aisle, and see a typical Gh woman standing there, there was a seat in front of me empty, she apologizes to the other passengers and says to me " "you don't mind?", I knobbed a no with my head, but knew that this was not goanna be a fun conversation, "how are you?" She asks, "sorry, but i don't recognize you right away" i said "we had a good party, me, with two girlfriends and you, downstairs behind Singel" I look at her bleached face and shiny wig and that weird pink lipstick and behold that gap between her front teeth, I think, yes, it was you " we never see you anymore" she says, I must have looked at her at that moment, couldn't help it, with dislike, and I said, "no i am busy" she "oh if you want

I can give you my phone number, i live in Almere now, you got phone"? No, no number, forgot, only foreign number. She opens her bag to find paper and pen, and continues, " you know, "i still thank God that he brought you to me" me " God?" " yes , i am very religious" as i watch a cheap version of michaela jackson, suddenly i remember,, ¡ it was you, you prepared a base pipe and pushed me to smoke it!!. She continues" me and my girlfriends talk many times about you", I think of course you do, dividing 27 grand by 3 is 9 grand for such pulled from under a corrugated roof curb side Ghanaian prostitute like you. You don't normally get this kind of money together in 9 years. Meanwhile, she had written her number on a tissue with her pink lipstick and placed it on the windowsill between us, "*here for you, i work Friday, Saturday and Wednesday.*"

What a concrete plate that woman must have had in front of her face, I felt my face glow with shame and hatred almost, I say, *"you really think God brought me too you "I honestly think you pray to the wrong God"* She looks at me with a questioning look on her face.. me:*" it was the devil who brought me to you, the devil and nobody else!"*, I couldn't stand it anymore, got up and walked all the way to the other side of the train.

It took me years to understand that when you go to the prostitutes and you abuse drugs like i did, and you think its all so incredible horny, i can guarantee you that you are the only one in that room who thinks it's horny, for them its just money, these lady's see you as an object, an opportunity to rake in some serious cash, nothing more, nothing less, some even hate men/clients I noticed, maybe that's why many are digging more girls than men, fact is that prostitutes are often damaged individuals who often come from broken homes and have suffered physical and/or mental abuse. Apart for a few working nymphomaniacs, but it's not difficult to imagine that when they have the umpteenth client in front of the door they also have to put an act together. In general prostitutes don't get turned on when they have sex with a client, nothing strange, I dated for a while a "working girl" who told me she had 20 clients or more a day, and every of these men after he take his pocket out expects his bag to be emptied and yes first pocket empty than bag, because prostitution is one of the only, if not the only profession that you have to pay in full in advance, " how does that feel?" i asked to my girlfriend at the time, "nothing" she said her pussy felt more like a "hole" it's more like a money pit, south American prostitutes call their pussy "very appropriate" an tarjeta credito", a credit card. I know men who go often to the prostitutes don't like to hear this, they like to believe otherwise and I always hear some say "I know plenty of girls who are really horny", well i say, "keep on dreaming", some of them just act better than others. There are also men who are addicted going to prostitutes without consuming substances, gives all sorts. While sitting on the terrace of our bar I've seen them coming and going, very ordinary men, some coming straight from the office with their attaché suitcase getting laid before going back to the misses, many of them even made a stop in our bar, going to the toilet to look if there was no lipstick visible I guess, most have one favorite, some a few, but most men are always looking for a "fresh" girl that just started to work, inexperienced and hopefully easy to manipulate. With what goal is for everybody different, i do know a few guys who tried to persuade these new girls to have sex without condom and though they learn very quick but with an experienced girl you can mostly forget that. And to look for that one new "green behind her ears" girl they walk literarily daily threw the red light, obsessed looking for that one opportunity. From the thousands of times i went to the prostitutes i can remember a hand full of occasions that when i left and thought, tjee, my goodness, was that for real or what? as said there are several that i will never forget one in particular, she was from Caribbean/English descent and worked maybe 1 or 2 years, definitely an attractive woman with all the curves in

310

the right place, for some extra money she did a lot, she worked in the evenings behind a lower window on the canal, I hadn't seen her for a while and when I walked past again I thought, "Gosh, she gained weight, i knock on the door, once inside, *"what's happened to you?" calories? no i am pregnant... what? yes really.* I took a look from close by , felt her belly...and damn it's true, of course this is sexually an opportunity , , so i asked her to close the curtain and we agreed on a price higher than normal and i asked her how long she wanted to continue working pregnant, she said she was 4 months pregnant and that she had never been as busy in the last few months as she has been ever before, she easily made 1500 per day she said, she would work for 1 more month and then stop for good and of course did the expectant father not mind that Johnny Doe and everyone were banging the front door of his soon-to-be child , and before the month was over i indeed went several times the pervert who i am, and indeed most of the times i had to wait, curtain closed.

But besides a hand full of occasions realizing that its all fake was very important in my recovery,, What I also tried to do, which is anything but easy, is to look at my behavior as an outsider, an independent person, so as if this writing belonged to someone else, it may be obvious that if you read such a book by this or that person that this person has a massive addiction problem, so reading it back, again and again, and see the sheer madness of it all, it helps because in fact the old you must be broken down spiritually

There was also something that happened that made me more reserved, something that everyone should take into account in this digital time we are living in and what I've found out, a lot happens in the world of prostitution, you are secretly getting filmed, this is done for various purposes, just by any prostitute with the aim of promotion, for example, there are plenty of images on certain famous Xxxx sites of clients who enter a prostitute place completely unsuspectingly and start doing their "thing"

Then there are those who exploit it economically in the same way and put it on their only fans website, and get paid per view, but again many times the client is unaware of being recorded

And then you have organized groups that secretly film you and then try to extort you.

This is what happened to me. Very spicy images of a grown man who is completely off the map on illicit drugs and is rambling around with a big dildo in his hand and much more.

-not exactly images that you like to go viral- There was a whole organization behind it i found out later, there were hidden cameras from different angles, the prostitute was obviously complicit, but also the "lady" of the house was in it.

Once the footages are in their possession another group joins in and tries to find out as much as possible about your private life via among others social media.

Once they obtain that the extortion starts, by receiving weird messages with part of the footages in question.

I told them to f*^#k themselves and took certain measurements to minimize the damage, and a "good" thing is that most people already know what craziness I do when on alcohol and illicit drugs

But still knowing and actually seeing are two totally different perceptions of course.

 At the end the extortion was not successful and the images have partly gone viral, and how they did this is mindboggling, for this they got other individuals, but unfortunately I cant reveal in this stage how they did this,   all in all gave a lot of headache, for what? Again to satisfy some b.s addiction, though i did loose some " friends" over it

This kind of practice happens more and more so if you're an avid whore runner, keep this in mind by knowing who you're doing "business" with.

For me it was a blessing because when the monkey tapped on my shoulder again I was suddenly much more restrained, thinking back on this event, mostly i started looking for alternatives that were not available to end up not doing it at all

Fact is that my life today would have looked totally different, without exaggeration I would be a multimillionaire now if i had never run into my addiction, or at least resisted the temptation, anything, something, but I didn't, I was helpless, I should have made the decision very early on to change my life a hundred and eighty degrees, but all should have, could have would have stories, and really nobody gives a f#&*k what you had, its all about what you have now here, because if all the if's and the buts were candy and nuts every day would be Christmas.

What I also found out is the lack of a father figure for a young man is indispensable, does not necessarily have to be your own father, uncle, neighbor, it does not matter, a person who commands respect, a person who acts as a guide in difficult issues in the life of a young man, i think the lack of a person like that was a great loss for me.

For the ones who don't know it yet, but with working a person doesn't get rich, I don't want to discourage anyone to work but the reality is not even with an above average wage of for example 50.000, or even 100.000, yeah sure a comfortable life, but when you have to sustain a family with a few kids it isn't much, working is except for ceo's or directors of multinationals who are making millions a year, but that's an extremely small percentage, your own business, assets, a niche/ invention or "making money with money" can make you rich, investing in stock or bonds in case you got a Chrystal boll but the reality is that that's privileged for the happy few, I tried it a few times, investing in shares, in this case oil, around beginning of April 2020, the oil went down to below 20 $ a barrel, I thought and many with me, that can only go up, so I invested for me at that moment a considerable amount of money in it, and on the 20th of the same month a historical event happened, oil went to minus -37 $!! a barrel, money gone, so for ordinary people the main money maker are assets, buying a house, when possible a few and having patience, and exactly that bit "among other things" I screwed up.

Believe me knowing I had access to mental money, I made millions and at a moment in life I had to bag for money is …hard,. No actually its ballistic mental, but in fact that deep I had to go, on my knees and even deeper to understand what a baboon I've been most of my life.

Maybe I even deserved it, I knew better than anyone, felt like I was king bobo from the Ukubuku tribe, i made a ton of money but i spanked faster as it came in, not only on prostitutes, i also loved consumer goods, basically anything i was always on a buyer spree mood, made me happy for a moment, but it was all a quick fix, going out for dinner with a beautiful woman, going to the prostitutes, buying a new car even, in hindsight a sign I was spiritually totally eroded.

I do know when I get a million tomorrow, I am on a slippery slope, good thing is I am aware of that fact, I know my limitations, so I can take the necessary precautions, I created over the years a whole protocol full of steps for myself. Among other things, I have a child lock on all my electronic devices, so that I can't watch porn or visit dating sites In any case, when you catch yourself watching porn on your electronic devices on a more than regular base it is really worth protecting your phone, watching too much porn is sickening, pathetic and more harmful than you think, it's ridiculous that everyone including children only having to click that they are older than 18 and then see the most vulgar sex, especially if you draw the comparison that if you post something politically different that doesn't fit the current narrative you will be blocked or banned, furthermore banking apps are on a separate phone and that phone is only accessible during certain hours, I have no alcohol at home, no alcohol is consumed at my house, not by anyone, whorehouses or red light districts are off limits, I don't even make an appointment within a radius of at least 5 km, nothing wrong with a protocol, only thing is it works till a certain extend, keeping drinking and once you are on the "marching powder" you'll find a way around that beautiful protocol, with other words the core of your problem stays, so absolute sobriety is the only way, there is simply no other way, no protocol nothing, unless protocol states "total abstinence of anything"

I could also have also called this book the A,B,C book, or actually A,B,C,D book, A for Alcohol, from A comes B for Booze {handbrakes gone} , from B comes C for Cocaine, {footbrakes gone} and then we go to D for Delusional nutcase, { no brakes at all even emergency brake gone} after all, that's how it is with many who are sensitive to addictions

But when you stay absent of any substances it is at least in my case you don't go along that path and emotions you "drink away" like   regret, hate, anything you don't like to get confronted with will take the upper hand, but you have to deal with it, its got all to do with your path to recovery, it will be difficult but there is a lot of power coming from sobriety

My regret was so deep that I had to find the balance between regret and not getting depressed, I could live a comfortable life now, very comfortable even looking back at the shit loads of money i made and now i have to scrape by, I lost the reality about the value of money, totally clueless about what money was worth, and if you don't respect money, money won't respect you either, i fell short to myself and my loved ones, acted very selfishly, especially looking at my children now who don't live in   particular a privileged life either, and last but not least   I last part of my vision in my right eye which is caused according to the doctor by extreme high blood pressure, [burst capillary] It happened when i came home after yet another wild night and when I opened the fridge I suddenly had a big grey spot in my eye which is still there up till today,

I have to always remember i am an addict it's in bedded in your system its like almost if your genes are modified.

When i joined the first gatherings from the N.A they told me clearly I have to stay absent from everything, including alcohol.

"But I am not an alcoholic" I said to the old school members of the first N.A meetings I joined, As I described earlier I attended meetings of the NA, AA and the S.L.A.A clearly because I couldn't put my finger on where my problem was, after all, I wasn't an alcoholic, I drank, but not the amounts that I faced physical problems from it, so I didn't see myself as an alcoholic, and I probably wasn't, but because I didn't see that alcohol was at the core of my self-destructive behavior, not seeing or admitting to that fact, very treacherous this behavior loomed on and was able to profile itself for yet another 15 years leaving a trail of destruction, that's why this little footnote, the earlier on you decide to change the less sour the apple is you have to eat, recovery is for a part beautiful but most definitely also biting threw the sour apple, and the longer you pros pone "your change" the more financial, social and collateral damage, the more damage the more regret, the more regret the more sour the apple, concerning alcohol I am convinced that occasionally consuming alcohol has much greater consequences for certain people than for those who pour a portion of alcohol into their bodies on a daily basis and are according to the holy grail the real alcoholics, so I wasn't an alcoholic following the holy grail criteria, but because of that assumption I kept that imaginary carrot in front of me for years and did not realize that by being absent from alcohol I reduced the chance of that self-

319

destructive behavior by 99% and besides that by being absent from alcohol I would allow myself to unravel spiritually and find out why I had this self-destructive behavior in the first place, Addiction in any form is the result of a psychic and spiritual emptiness Traumas, mostly passed on from generation to generation. We incur most traumas in our youth, with all the consequences that entails later in life: social isolation and loneliness, stress, fear and ultimately that addictive dependence. You have to understand that with what I've been through, seen from people around me, I can now say that I'm an expert at saying "how (not) to do it" in life, and came to the conclusion that though I never enjoyed them myself neither implemented them but traditional family values as they are described in the bible, among other things, are very close to my heart, I know now the well-known family cornerstone is indispensable.

CHILDREN, OBEY YOUR PARENTS IN THE LORD, FOR THIS IS RIGHT. "HONOR YOUR FATHER AND MOTHER" (THIS IS THE FIRST COMMANDMENT WITH A PROMISE), "THAT IT MAY GO WELL WITH YOU AND THAT YOU MAY LIVE LONG IN THE LAND." FATHERS, DO NOT PROVOKE YOUR CHILDREN TO ANGER, BUT BRING THEM UP IN THE DISCIPLINE AND INSTRUCTION OF THE LORD.

EPHESIANS 6: 1-4

_____ *"Big game fishing"*

I had come to a very dark period in my life, at the time I hadn't seen my kids for years, I was drinking almost every day and I was totally skinned, [no money] I could not even pay the rent at a certain moment, and was again (though very rarely) out of control concerning drug abuse, I ended up in a deep dark hole, a vicious circle, drunk, depressed no hope, miserable, couldn't take it anymore, started to have suicidal thoughts, there was simply in my perspective no hope, nothing.. I got consumed by my past, the gigantic mess I had made of it all, the ridiculous amount of money I had spanked, I just wanted to step out, and started to make plans how I was going to do that -stepping out of life- I thought of hanging myself, but didn't fancy a rope around my neck, and what if it did not work? the thought of suffocation, no, maybe jumping from a building? But I am seriously afraid of heights, no problem with helicopters, air balloons or planes, been in them all, but fixed objects, buildings, steep walls, ravines and mountain ridges and I put it in my pants, so after deliberation it had to be a bullet, that's the solution, but not at home, when my daughter is there to say goodbye for the last time, that's all to emotional, for her, for the neighborhood, I knew a friend who during a house eviction had found a gun, he had shown it to me, some kind of luger, an antique weapon from the second world war, although the thing looked like it belonged once to Napoleon, he wanted 400€ for it, I told him I had a customer, a blatant lie of course, so I picked it up from him, there were two bullets left in the clip, then I went to another friend who lives right on the beach who owns a fishing kayak, and asked if I could borrow it for a fishing trip which I had done before, he agreed and I went out to sea on a beautiful calm and sunny autumn day the sea was like a mirror, so I paddled for at least an hour away from the coast, it must have been about 5 or 6 km, I looked back, It was far out from the shore, I waited for a commercial fishing boat to pass by, and grabbed the luger, I loaded it up, and waited until the fishing boat was far enough away so that they couldn't hear the bang, I looked closely at the gun and thought, does this thing actually work? If it goes following plan I only need one bullet to blow my brains out, I had two, so I aimed at a piece of wreckage nearby and pulled the trigger...BANG...and a big plume of water, clearly it worked, it was time, my last minute on planet earth had arrived, I looked at the sky and put the barrel in my mouth...than suddenly I thought ill do it differently, I put it on my temple and leaned to the right with my elbow in the water, I think because of my dislike for the authorities, I thought I'm going to leave them a riddle, a homicide or suicide riddle, the moment I pull the trigger the thing will fall from my hand and plunge into the sea, before they find me I may have already drifted hundreds of meters or more away from the "crime scene", with that luger somewhere at the bottom of the sea, and let them figure it out, the kayak had not only a fish finder but also a depth gauge, I look its 18 meters, I look into the sea, the water was crystal clear, you could easily see meters down, no I thought, they'll maybe find it, so I paddle further out, watching the depth gauge, it rises, 30, 35, gradually it goes up, until suddenly its at 66 meters, I grab the luger again, lean to the right, put it against my temple, and look at the gun again to see if I took off the safety catch, yes I did, while looking at the gun I see that the registration number has partly been filed away, one number was still visible, 6, gosh I think, look at the depth gauge again, still on 66 meters deep, how is that, a 6 on the weapon and normally while floating the depth is continuously changing, it stayed exactly on 66 meter, 6 on the gun, 66 meter deep, 666.. Satan's number came to my mind, then something very strange happened, it was like something "terrestrial" like another entity took possession of my thoughts, and threw my own voice it said

"You don't want this, the devil wants this, you're not doing this for yourself, you're doing this for him, he takes pleasure in it, leading your loved ones into grief, you came to a crossroad in your life today, and it went on and on, the same thing over and over crossroad, crossroad, crossroad, make the right decision, right decision, right decision, change and you'll be saved, be saved, be saved. So you change? Was what was popped up in my head, and over and over, I said in myself, yes of course I change, but not really meaning it, knowing a change is a giant step, so this went on for a while, and every time I promised I'll change but actually didn't mean it I started to feel more and more uncomfortable, my heart was racing and it felt like I got a hyper-ventilation attack, it actually felt even like I overdosed on cocaine once again, it got worse and worse and seriously panicked if maybe I a am in danger of an heart attack here where it felt like I was in the middle of the ocean, -how weird is that? You're there to take your own life, but afraid of a heart attack.

I got drawn back to the 66 mtr spot and looked at the gun, and heard...do it!!, blow your brains out here! Now! Don't matter 66 or not, just do it!

It became clear when I wouldn't change after i go back to shore I'll certainly be back in a similar situation in a matter of weeks and guaranteed it doesn't matter on which depth the gauge is than, its going to be end of story for me, the choice was up to me, this spiritual awakening seemed like it took many hours, but later it turned out it didn't last more than maybe ten minutes, it was an unbelievable experience, so intense that it's impossible to describe. I thought f*#^k all this, ..I'm doing this for myself, and for no one else! and certainly not for the devil! I put the gun away again and felt tricked, fooled, by whom? I didn't really know, but I paddled back to the shore and in the mean time there was an struggle taking place within me with something that said, "come on mate, for what did you paddle out here in the first place? don't go back to that shitty miserable life!, just finish it of, its no big deal a bullet threw your head, and at same time... no, you can change and have a better life, paddle as fast you can to shore now, after what seemed that took hours, I paddled as fast as possible back and the further I got away from that that lets say 666 spot the better I started feeling, that anxiety feeling went away, pure relieve I felt, and thinking "what bull shit is all this, borrowing a gun in good faith from someone, someone who trusts me that I can sell that thing on for him, but knowing the moment he gave me that gun that I was going to blow my brains out with it, and then on top of that making it a mystery by leaving a kind of "crime scene" behind? and then the man who lent me his kayak? what would he think about me for the rest of his life? Will he ever use it again?

I was just fooling myself and everybody around me.... a fishing trip?...are you kidding?! what will people think of me? my children and loved ones who sooner or later will hear all this...what a legacy to leave behind! worthless... once I arrived on the beach I pulled the kayak away from the waves, I knelt

326

beside it putting my elbows on the kayak and burying my head in my hands, and burst into tears, and really cried like I hadn't done in 40 years, and shouted "oh my god in heaven" or something along those lines, maybe something a lot of people would do in such a crisis situation like this, but this was different, I felt his presence, I knew there and then, he is here, I gave in to the love I felt, I was ripe, meanwhile a woman with a child came up to me with a paper tissue for my tears and asked if everything was alright with me, I nodded and smiled and said I was doing great, I brought the kayak back to my mate and he saw me coming from a distance while sitting on his terrace he said" you look happy you must have caught a really big one? , .. yes, I said the biggest there is" I felt sucked empty, like I run a marathon and I had a strong feeling to read the bible, and asked him if there was a bookstore in the area, and bought a bible the same day, the King James version, making my way to my house I felt incredible tired but also so intense relieved, I actually felt happy, better than I had done in a long time and it ushered in the moment of a major change in my life, a change big enough to never go apeshit anymore in my life

ON THAT DAY YOU WILL REALIZE THAT I AM IN MY FATHER, AND YOU ARE IN ME, AND I AM IN YOU

The core of this whole book, most (not all) of us are as lost as those you call out as being stupid, inferior. Most (not all), have their heads in the sand right along with those you claim to detest, me included at times. This is all quite simple actually, but yet it is one of the most difficult decisions for many of us. All in life has been about good vs evil since the dawn of man. Nothing has changed in 6000 years since Adam and Eve were deceived in the garden. Satan is to blame for it all. He is the great deceiver; he has been pulling the strings of the world from the beginning. He already knows he has lost, but here is the catch. He knows he is doomed, so he wants to doom as many of us to hell as he can. That is pure hatred if you ask me. In his sick mind, that is how he wins. Like I said, he knows God wins, but not before he deceived individuals or even the whole world by having powerful individuals under his spell. Wake up, help those that need it, be kind to one another, Love one another, rejoice in the fact that God sent his only son to save us all. All you have to do is believe in him, that he died on the cross, and he rose on the third day, and repent of your sins. That is the true gospel. Like I said, it is a very difficult decision for some of us, and we will all fall short. Thy spirit is willing, but thy flesh is weak. There is so many worldly, fleshly, and materialistic temptation that will cause us to fall short. Don't let it, fight it with all your might. Stand strong as possible in the faith, pray for your enemies, forgive those that transgress, and be the best that he would want you to be.

In Jesus name, amen